Did Anyone Else See That Coming...?

# Did Anyone Else See That Coming...?

Unpublished Letters to
**The Daily Telegraph**

<small>EDITED BY</small>
<small>IAIN HOLLINGSHEAD WITH KATE MOORE</small>

Aurum
Press

Brimming with creative inspiration, how-to projects and useful information to enrich your everyday life, Quarto Knows is a favourite destination for those pursuing their interests and passions. Visit our site and dig deeper with our books into your area of interest: Quarto Creates, Quarto Cooks, Quarto Homes, Quarto Lives, Quarto Drives, Quarto Explores, Quarto Gifts, or Quarto Kids.

First published in 2017 by Aurum Press
an imprint of The Quarto Group
The Old Brewery, 6 Blundell Street
London N7 9BH
United Kingdom

www.QuartoKnows.com

Copyright © 2017 Telegraph Media Group
Introduction copyright © 2017 Iain Hollingshead

Iain Hollingshead and Kate Moore have asserted their moral right to be identified as the Editors of this Work in accordance with the Copyright Designs and Patents Act 1988.

A catalogue record for this book is available from the British Library.

ISBN 978 1 78131 699 3
Ebook ISBN 978 1 78131 765 5

10 9 8 7 6 5 4 3

2021 2020 2019 2018 2017

Typeset in Mrs Eaves by SX Composing DTP, Rayleigh, Essex

Printed by CPI Group (UK) Ltd, Croydon, CR0 4YY

FSC
www.fsc.org
MIX
Paper from
responsible sources
FSC® C020471

SIR – I have just finished the eighth book of unpublished letters and need another to keep me sane before sleep each night.

**Jean Adams**
Charlbury, Oxfordshire

SIR – Give me some vintage cheese and biscuits, a decent bottle of red wine and the Letters page from *The Daily Telegraph* and I will die a happy man.

**Ian Cribb**
Poole, Dorset

# CONTENTS

# INTRODUCTION

It is interesting to consider what has changed in the nine years since I started editing these books of unpublished letters. Certainly, there are more letters about technology – not just the perennial bugbears of mobile phones, dishwashers and toasters that don't work, but also brand new concerns about everything from drones to driverless cars (how will they know how to pass each other on country lanes?), the Twitter account of the President of the United States to sex robots (do they, too, get headaches?). One correspondent writes this year to share her fear that her Amazon Echo might be trying to murder her. *Telegraph* readers do their best to keep up with the modern world, even if it does not always meet with their full approval.

Conversely, there are far fewer letters these days about naughty bankers, phone hackers, footballers, Pippa Middleton, Jeremy Clarkson, the Armed Forces and wind farms – although in the last case, this might be due to an editorial blindness to this most tedious of subjects. Over the course of a decade, the readers have welcomed two American Presidents, several new members of the Royal Family and two British Prime Ministers, with varying degrees of enthusiasm, while trying – and failing – to wean themselves off writing about Tony Blair and Gordon Brown. In only one edition was there nothing about the latter, whereas his nemesis can now boast the dubious honour of having being abused nine years in a row. Perhaps he doesn't help himself.

What I am most struck by, however, is the sense of whimsical continuity across the editions. Yes, the world might seem a more dangerous place than it has been for three decades, yet *Telegraph* letter-writers are still principally concerned by more important topics — such as whether the fruit in Pimm's constitutes part of their five-a-day, the BBC's incorrect pronunciation of *harassment*, and whether they have had more letters published in the newspaper than their neighbours.

Of course, this is not to say that *Telegraph* readers inhabit a bubble that is untouched by the dizzying 24-hour news cycle. Here, too, they are more than adept at providing their own refreshing angle. Why is it that North Korea can produce nuclear weapons, but no decent barbers? Has anyone actually tried running through a wheat field, as Theresa May daringly admitted (jolly painful, apparently)? Who can get the words "strong and stable" into the most number of domestic situations? How large would your heating bill have to be to be able to afford to wear Samantha Cameron's sleeveless garments? Might Jacob Rees-Mogg's nanny be prepared to join him in the Cabinet? Shouldn't Jeremy Corbyn remove his Breton-style headwear now that Britain has voted for Brexit? And has anyone else noticed how well *Juncker* and *Tusk* serve as ersatz swear words? In these uncertain times, *Telegraph* letter-writers have shown their true mettle.

Behind the scenes, you might already have noticed one change on the cover. I am grateful to Kate Moore who, after helping last year with the initial legwork for the book, sorting through the wheat and the chaff as it arrived, produced an early draft of this edition. It has, I believe, benefitted hugely from her keen eye and expert editing. It also allows me to make a more convincing innocent plea to any charge of nepotism, having discovered, quite by chance, that two people I know personally have made it into the book.

As always, I am also grateful to Matt, Christopher Howse, the Letters Editor, everyone at Aurum Press and, of course, to the incomparable letter-writers themselves. No one, least of all highly paid commentators, appears to be able to predict the twists and turns of the news cycle at the moment. But if the readers didn't see it coming, they always know exactly what to say when it does.

**Iain Hollingshead**
London SE22

# FAMILY LIFE AND TRIBULATIONS

# WEDDED BLITZ

SIR – My parents were married on 3 September and my father always referred to their wedding day as "the day war broke out".

**Trina Golland**
Hatfield, Hertfordshire

SIR – True love is when your other half offers to slice the onions. My wife does so and has not shed a tear since the day I proposed to her.

**Philip Dawson**
Dorking, Surrey

SIR – It is getting more and more difficult to find a special gift for the special person in your life. Do you think it would be wise to ring my ex-wife for advice?

**Roger St Taw**
Walsall, West Midlands

SIR – A colleague once told me he was buying his wife an electric carving knife for Christmas.

I suggested it would not be a good start to Christmas morning.

"Oh no," he said. "She'll not get it until after the sales start."

**Peter J. Beckett**
Bromley, Kent

SIR – Over 40 years ago, when we were first married, my husband bought me a pension book wallet for Christmas.

Now that it is coming near to a time when it could be of use, I cannot find it. Unfortunately his present-buying skills have not improved.

**Lesley Ball**
Liskeard, Cornwall

SIR — My husband is highly intellectual. I found it difficult to interrupt his musings until just recently, when, thanks to *University Challenge*, I have discovered a new technique for getting his attention: "I'm Mary, I'm from Heysham and [whatever needs to be said]."

**Mary Gibson**
Heysham, Lancashire

SIR — I am considering writing a book called *I Married a Dysfunctional Robot*.

**Sheina Burns**
Shaw, Lancashire

SIR — My wife woke up this morning and decided she would spend the morning making a cake. A little while later she said she had changed her mind, as I would only eat it.
     Life is strange, isn't it?

**Michael A. Mills**
Appledore, Devon

SIR — In March this year I will have been married for 33 years. Today my wife complained that I put too much milk in her coffee. Why has it taken her nigh on 35 years to complain?

**G. Brown**
Manchester

SIR – It does not matter if you are henpecked, provided you are pecked by a good hen.

**John Croft**
Henfield, West Sussex

SIR – My wife complains that I do not kiss her enough. Is this the time for inventing fish-and-chip-flavoured lipstick?

**Douglas Iles**
Stanford-le-Hope, Essex

SIR – For Valentine's Day I bought my wife a defibrillator. It seems to cover all bases.

**Piers Casimir-Mrowczynski**
Gustard Wood, Hertfordshire

SIR – Has the age of consent been lowered without my noticing? My Valentine card to "A Wonderful Wife" has a note printed on the back: "Warning. Not suitable for children under 36 months".

**Olwyn Venn**
Norwich

# READING, WRITING AND REPRODUCTION

SIR – You report that schools are to provide extra sex education. In view of the low levels of numeracy among our youth, could we please have some emphasis on addition, subtraction and division, as well as multiplication?

**Geoffrey Cullington**
Dorchester, Dorset

SIR — The recent controversy about sex education reminds me of a training course I once attended where one of the participants asked what the difference was between education and training.

The tutor replied by saying: "If your young daughter comes home from school and says, 'We had sex education today', you might think, good — that saves me a job. On the other hand, if she says, 'We had sex training today', you would be horrified."

I've always thought that sums it up pretty well.

**Barry Graham**
Upton, Cheshire

SIR — When I was at Marlborough in the 1950s, the Master decided that we should meet more girls.

Consequently a notice went up saying "Dancing vs St Mary's Calne".

**Tim Le Blanc-Smith**
London SW18

SIR — "A study finds older women have more chance of conceiving with a youthful chap."

As a breeder of rabbits during the war, I could have told them that off the cuff.

**Ron Hurrell**
Benfleet, Essex

# #NOTTONIGHTTHANKYOUDEAR

SIR – Readers must have read your article about sex robots and wondered: Will they have headaches?

> **Vivian Bush**
> Hessle, East Yorkshire

SIR – You report that sex will only be for special occasions in the future. I believe the future is already here. I call it getting married and having children.

> **Andrew Holgate**
> Woodley, Cheshire

SIR – We read with interest the article about having sex every day for 14 days. As I said to my wife, it might do us good to cut down for a while.

> **Malcolm Holland**
> Billericay, Essex

SIR – You report that women over 80 enjoy sex more than younger women. Oh, to have been a witness at just a few breakfast tables to see the reactions from both partners.

> **Alan Cubbin**
> Weasenham Saint Peter, Norfolk

SIR – I read that 90 per cent of *Cosmopolitan* readers had taken a naked selfie.

Would anyone like to guess how many *Daily Telegraph* readers had done the same?

> **Michael Morris**
> Christchurch, Dorset

# APPROPRIATE OFFICE BEHAVIOUR

SIR – The *Telegraph* carries a report on a dentist who apparently "carried out inappropriate sexual relations in his office".

Call it simple prurience on my part, but I (and, no doubt, quite a number of people who work in offices) would find it helpful to be told what constitutes appropriate sexual relations for carrying out in the office.

Perhaps it could be published next winter, ahead of the office party season.

**Graeme W.I. Davidson**
Edinburgh

# HOW MANY SLEEPS UNTIL CHRISTMAS?

SIR – At the weekend I asked an elderly relative, who still gets excited about Christmas, how many "sleeps" there were until the big day. She wasn't familiar with the expression but soon caught on. Referring to her husband's propensity to doze off after lunch and during the evening, she said in his case it would be around two hundred.

**David Miller**
Tunbridge Wells, Kent

# HAPPY SNOWMAN DAY

SIR – I was offered a choice of Christmas stamps at my local post office: "Either the snowmen ones, or the ones with a lady on."

The young man behind the counter was quite bemused when I was able to name the lady: Mary. I could name the baby, too.

**Dr Lynda Taylor**
Bury, Lancashire

SIR — I once overheard a young woman gazing at plastic crucifixes in a seaside souvenir shop ask the assistant if they had any with the little bloke on.

**B.S.**
Chorleywood, Hertfordshire

SIR — My late father-in-law, who spent most of his working life in the Far East, was invited to the unveiling of a Christmas tableau in a large department store in Japan.

He was never able to erase from his memory the image of the curtains parting to reveal the crucifixion of Father Christmas.

**Nicolas Robertson**
London SW13

SIR — Displayed in my local supermarket: "Christmas Mince Pies". And on the packets: "Use by November 26".

**Jane Hemsley**
Northwich, Cheshire

SIR — We received a Christmas card from my husband's cousin last Christmas. In it he'd written: "Please don't bother to send us your newsletter again. Our lives are so much more interesting than yours."

We have taken the hint.

**J.A.**
Chatham, Kent

SIR — A retired schoolmaster friend of mine last year received an unsigned and un-postmarked Christmas card, with the cryptic message "Looking forward to seeing you next year!"

Since then he has daily hoped it had not been sent by the Grim Reaper.

**Elizabeth Lee**
Merstham, Surrey

# HIGHLIGHTS OF A LONG LIFE

SIR — I told a friend that I was too old to drown; it would take so long for my life to pass before my eyes that I would have time to walk to shore along the bottom.

She helpfully suggested that my life might pass before my eyes in the form of edited highlights.

Now scientists have found that this is, in fact, the arrangement, I suppose I must learn to swim — or perhaps have more highlights.

**John Hart**
Chelmsford, Essex

SIR — I see that we have yet another report recommending that old fogeys like me should stand up every 20 minutes.

Don't they realise that it takes me that long to stand up?

**John Jenkins**
Bath

SIR — I note that scientists are calling for more people to donate their brains to research.

They are more than welcome to mine — if only I could remember where I put it.

**Michael West**
Amesbury, Wiltshire

SIR — "Brushing teeth could prevent heart attacks", according to your headline.

Does it matter whether the teeth are in the mouth or not?

**Barbara Loryman**
Weedon, Buckinghamshire

SIR — You report that Judith Kerr, the children's author, recommends that people carry a note to convey "do not resuscitate" wishes — or perhaps a tattoo — when they get to 75.

I had the same idea about a tattoo, but when I mentioned it to my daughters, the younger one said it would be no good because doctors would have to iron me first.

So I'm going for a necklace.

**Sarah Smith**
Deal, Kent

SIR — Having reached my early seventies, I am wondering about signs of advancing senility among my friends, one of whom I watched yesterday, after a pub lunch, patiently holding his wet hands beneath a rectangular white cabinet bolted to the wall in the gentlemen's lavatory, waiting for hot air.

The only problem was that it was a paper towel dispenser.

Are there other significant signs to start watching out for?

> **C.S.M. Mitchell**
> Houghton on the Hill, Leicestershire

SIR – I will reach my 62nd birthday in August. Can anyone tell me when I might expect to suffer my mid-life crisis?

> **Steven Broomfield**
> Fair Oak, Hampshire

SIR – Having attained my 70th birthday, I am being told that I don't look it. What a disappointment. Do I need to dress from head to foot in fawn clothes?

> **Keith Rowlands**
> Shirenewton, Monmouthshire

SIR    Twice recently, when giving payment details by phone, I've been asked for my expiry date. Hopefully it is considerably longer than that of my credit card.

> **Jean Renshaw**
> Kingswood, Surrey

SIR – Why is it that so many cruise holidays to exotic, far-flung destinations seem to be advertised as the "ultimate" trip of a lifetime?

As we enter the twilight years of our lives, the "penultimate" equivalents would be of much greater interest to me and my wife.

> **Bruce Chalmers**
> Goring-by-Sea, West Sussex

SIR — I, along with the rest of my contemporaries, will downsize in the next five to ten years without the need to move to smaller housing. We will reside in a box in the ground or become part of the atmosphere via the crematorium chimney.

Be patient!

**Brian C. Roberts**
Fulwood, Lancashire

SIR — What can I do to become an inmate at HMP Berwyn? It offers better facilities and is probably cheaper than a care home.

As a former Royal Marine, I will have a rapport with the Governor.

**B.G. Woolvine**
Corfe Mullen, Dorset

SIR — My father, Togo, did strenuous exercises every day, ate moderately and drank very little alcohol. He was so anxious to keep up his regime that, aged 73, he prepared for a spell in hospital by getting ahead with his exercises, doing them twice a day for three months.

His brother Walter eschewed exercise, was a great trencherman and loved his drink.

Dad died aged 78. Uncle Walter survived into his 90th year. Whose example should I follow?

**John Bromley-Davenport**
Malpas, Cheshire

# FIT KNIT

SIR — My wife has discovered that she can achieve 10,000 steps while wearing her wrist pedometer and sitting on the sofa knitting.

**Andrew Rance**
Basingstoke, Hampshire

SIR — A year or two ago I read a flyer for Nordic walking poles which assured me that I would burn 20 per cent more calories.

I decided to forgo the experience and thus travel 20 per cent further per Mars Bar.

**Marcus Croome**
Truro, Cornwall

# THE THIN OF THE LAND

SIR — I was intrigued to read the statement from Professor Steve Jones claiming that a raw-food diet "will kill you in months".

My "nutty sister", as we kindly call her, has been living off the land, eating raw food only, somewhere in the French wilderness for over 40 years. She has been trying very hard to convince the rest of our family that we've got it all wrong. She hasn't had much luck.

There is one advantage: they are no bother when they visit. They arrive with a van packed with crates full of fruit, vegetables and nuts.

**Rosmarie Hall**
Canterbury

SIR — Kale is disgusting and really only fit for cattle or celebrities.

**Christopher Seaton**
Sidmouth, Devon

SIR — I have to admit that I am completely indifferent to Marmite. Does this mean that I have a problem?

**T.W.D. Smith**
Sheffield

SIR — Scientists have suggested that it may be possible to genetically modify quinoa to create a superfood that is destined to feed the world. This seems a long way away when half the world cannot spell *quinoa* and the other half cannot pronounce it.

**Clive Pilley**
Westcliff-on-Sea, Essex

SIR — Why don't people who consume "energy" drinks have the stamina to bin or take home their empties?

**Hugh Wiseman**
Saffron Walden, Essex

SIR — I think gulls should be encouraged to steal food from people eating in the street.

**Ian McMullen**
Doddington, Kent

SIR — I have been imbibing a generous daily dosage of high-strength fish oil for some 20 years and have rarely been subject to heavy colds or flu.

There have been few side-effects, including possibly a slight scaliness of the skin, but swimming has become effortless.

**Barry Bond**
Leigh-on-Sea, Essex

SIR — In January, when every expert is giving us their foolproof diet and exercise regime, are not the words at the end of every such article — "Please check with your doctor before starting any diet or exercise" — somewhat strange?

The utopian idea of having a cosy 30-minute chat with our GP about the relative merits of the 5:2 or the total fasting diet — or what type of exercise he most favours — is frankly pie-in-the-sky.

By the time you even get the appointment in three weeks' time you will have lost the will to live, never mind diet.

**Gay Rhodes**
Cheadle Hulme, Cheshire

SIR — Following reports that every cup of coffee consumed prolongs life by nine minutes, if one drinks the coffee in less than nine minutes and continues to do so uninterrupted, immortality would seem to be guaranteed — plumbing difficulties notwithstanding.

**James Omer**
Shotteswell, Oxfordshire

SIR — Such is the present depressing state of governance in this country that I am sorely tempted to cease consuming coffee.

**Frank Felton**
Stapleford, Cambridgeshire

SIR — Everybody eats. Everybody dies. Food is bad for you.

**Harry Wood**
Manchester

SIR — There were doughnuts in the staffroom on my first day at work as a new graduate in 1984. It was a huge boost to my confidence when I learnt they were to celebrate my arrival. The next day there were doughnuts to celebrate a member of staff's birthday. The next day there were doughnuts to celebrate the beautiful Plymouth April weather. The next day there were doughnuts . . .

**Sally Goulden**
Ashford, Middlesex

SIR — Dietary requirements have finally reached the Church of England. Last Sunday my wife overheard a member of the congregation at our local parish church ask a warden if the communion wafers were gluten-free.

**Philip Samengo-Turner**
Cirencester, Gloucestershire

# FIVE POTIONS A DAY

SIR — To increase my consumption of fruit and vegetables, I intend to drink more Pimm's.

**Jennie Gibbs**
Goring-by-Sea, West Sussex

SIR — My grandmother pushed her empty glass towards her adult granddaughter and announced: "My usual."

To which the response was: "And the magic word is?" My grandmother's reply: "Whisky."

**Gay Wilmot-Smith**
North Marston, Buckinghamshire

SIR — Whenever my late, bibulous father was asked in restaurants whether he'd like some water, he invariably replied: "No, thanks, I've already washed."

**Charles Doxat**
London WI

SIR — I wish beer manufacturers would invent a silent ring-pull system for their cans. I'm fed up with the sound of the wife saying: "Oh, you're not having another one, are you?"

**Michael Cattell**
Mollington, Cheshire

# FAST WOMEN

SIR — It's reported that women are now drinking more than men, but it seems to me that they are also eating much faster than men. Every time I have taken a woman for a meal lately — particularly younger women — they are scraping their plates when I have hardly finished saying grace.

I am beginning to suspect that some kind of secret evolutionary race is going on here, and it worries me.

**Graham Masterton**
Tadworth, Surrey

# WHERE'S HARRY?

SIR – I have just bought some fruit from Waitrose. According to the labels, my strawberries were packed by Harry Hall in West Sussex, whereas my raspberries were packed by Harry Hall in Berkshire.

May I suggest that Mrs Hall keeps close tabs on Harry as he obviously gets about?

**Anthony Perrin**
Farnham, Surrey

# COSY TEA

SIR – All too often a pot of tea in a hotel or seaside café comes naked to the table. My hat then comes to the rescue, much to the embarrassment of my wife. As a bonus, I then have a nice warm hat to wear when venturing back outside.

**Andrew Baxter**
Banbury, Oxfordshire

# PISCES DE RESISTANCE

SIR – After long resistance I have been persuaded to try a dish of calamari and can only imagine the experience as akin to eating frittered gastric bands.

**John Allen**
Henley-on-Thames, Oxfordshire

SIR – It seems that most pubs are now referred to as gastropubs. Having been to quite a few I have come to the conclusion that in some the "gastro" seems to stand for gastronomic, whereas in others gastroenteritis would seem to be more appropriate.

**Richard Dalgleish**
Kingsclere, Berkshire

# ALES AND GRACES

SIR – A friend once ran a pub called the Duke of Hamilton. I called in one morning to find him chortling over a letter he had just received from the local Conservative association. It began "Your Grace . . ."
   He had it framed and hung in the public bar.

**Jane Cullinan**
Padstow, Cornwall

SIR – We have several charity shops in our town, but no charity pubs. Why is this?

**Philip Saunders**
Bungay, Suffolk

SIR – I lost half my right index finger in an accident as a young boy, and far from being a handicap, I have always found it enormously useful when attempting to order four and a half pints in a crowded and noisy bar.

**Graham Snowdon**
Sheffield

SIR – Seen on the side of a van belonging to the local pub: "No barmaids are kept in this van overnight".

**David Birkett**
Normanton, Nottinghamshire

SIR – Few of we that survive are able to recall with glowing pride those halcyon days when every public house in the land served only mild and bitter beers.

A recent private survey took me to more pubs in a week than I had visited in years. My request for a "Pint of bitter, please" was met with one of two responses: either "What is that?" or "Can you point to it?"

When I asked the whereabouts of the parlour or snug, the blank looks were sufficient to make an old soldier weep into his dimple.

**Edward Dunleavy**
Chesterfield, Derbyshire

SIR – Charles Moore quite rightly deplores swearing in pubs. When smoking was prohibited in 2007, enterprising landlords compensated by constructing outside shelters. Would it not be possible to provide those who insist on using bad language with a similar construction, perhaps with soundproofing, wherein they may exchange expletives without upsetting those of a sensitive disposition or children?

**C.D.**
Burton in Kendal, Cumbria

## LET THEM EAT TREATS

SIR — We had the most darling trick or treaters last night. One little girl proudly proclaimed herself to be a "zombie Marie Antoinette".

**Stephen Webbe**
East Molesey, Kent

## COLONEL (TIRED)

SIR — Our son asked our three-and-a-half-year-old grandson if he knew the meaning of "retired". "A little tired" came the confident reply.

**Colin T. Barrett**
West Wickham, Kent

SIR — I retired nearly 20 years ago, since when I have been so busy that I cannot imagine how I ever had time to go to work.

When I mentioned this a few years ago to my wife's uncle, who as the Dean of Windsor had recently retired, he commented that in his opinion retirement was a job for a much younger man.

**Richard Graves**
Canon Frome, Herefordshire

## DEPRESSED GRANDPARENTS

SIR — My husband avoided the depressing term *Grandad* by introducing *Pof*. The current translation is Pompous

Old Friend. Further translation will be forthcoming on puberty.

**E.P.**
Newbourne, Suffolk

SIR — We will be fostering a cat for a month or two while her staff goes abroad. As she shares her name (Millie) with our granddaughter, it will be interesting to see who comes first when called.

**Kay Clifton**
West Horsley, Surrey

SIR — Not only does looking after grandchildren add five years to your life, as you report, it makes it seem like ten.

**S.P.**
Bridgend

SIR — Having just had my first promotion to "Grandpa", I believe I now fully understand the difficulties of modern motherhood.

The contraptions that they have to deal with are excruciating. Pushchairs must be the worst. As an experienced engineer I could passably explain the theory of flight, jet engines and nuclear reactors, but I couldn't collapse the pushchair when I was left with the granddaughter.

Probably designed by a man.

**Michael West**
Bishopstoke, Hampshire

SIR – My three-year-old granddaughter calls me Gaga.
I am yet to discover if this is a term of endearment or an
assessment of my mental state.

**David Nunn**
West Malling, Kent

SIR – My grandchildren call me Hump. My stepdaughters
call me Faux Pa.

**P.R.**
Winchester

SIR – When our first grandson was born, my wife asked me
if I'd prefer to be called Grandpa or Grandad.
   I said, "Neither. I just want to be called Phil."
   My wife said, "Don't be silly. You can't be called Phil.
Why are you so always so grumpy? You can be called
Grumpy."
   And to this day, I'm "Grumpy".

**Phil Jones**
Cheltenham, Gloucestershire

SIR – There is a village called Old Sodbury in the
Cotswolds. Whenever we drive through my wife looks at me
and raises a knowing eyebrow.

**Dr Russell Steele**
Exeter

# AN R BY ANY OTHER NAME

SIR – A few years ago, when asked for my initials over the
phone, I replied "R for Robert".

Sure enough, next day I received a letter from the party concerned addressed to "Arthur Robert Cory".

**Robert Cory**
Altrincham, Cheshire

SIR — I was told by my history master that the correct way to declare your name on the telephone was without the prefix "mister". He told us that unless you had a specific title, the timbre of your voice should be enough to declare your sex. This has resulted in some people referring to me as Sir Mengo Turner.

**Philip Samengo-Turner**
Cirencester, Gloucestershire

# GENDER AGENDAS

SIR — You report that the London Underground is replacing the announcement "Ladies and gentlemen" as it's not gender-neutral. But apparently "guys" is.

**Edward Thomas**
Eastbourne, East Sussex

SIR — In 1958, when I was a cadet in the CCF, I can recall a fellow cadet telling me of an Army form that he had reason to complete, which had a tick box for Male and a tick box for Female.

Below these it said: "If neither, state both".
All of today's gender quandaries solved?

**Angus Jacobsen**
Inverbervie, Angus

SIR — I hate it when a shop assistant asks: "Is she (or he) your partner?"

No, mate, we've been married for 45 years and she's my wife (or husband) or, come to that, my mate.

Partners are the Lone Ranger and Tonto, or Torvill and Dean.

**Kevin Platt**
Walsall, West Midlands

# HELP TO BUY

SIR — Some years ago my wife sent me to her favourite supermarket with a long list, made in her characteristic recursive style, and not in any particular order. I sought the guidance of another man of mature years, who seemed pleased to be relieved of shelf-stacking duties. Together we worked our way down the list and back and forth between aisles, until we were left with one line, which appeared to be of four letters, of which the first appeared to be "s" and the last "t".

We agreed that it could not possibly read what one's first attempt made it. I decided it must read "suet", which is what I took home, to my wife's surprise.

She had written her version of "fruit".

**Christopher Macy**
Wellingore, Lincolnshire

SIR — I am disappointed that Tesco is about to ban the wearing of pyjamas in their stores. I was hoping that my husband could pop out for a bit of shopping in his night attire.

Could be a bit chilly around the freezers, mind, as he doesn't wear any.

> **Tricia Camm**
> Ruswarp, North Yorkshire

SIR — I have long thought that department stores should have male-only seating areas provided for husbands/ partners of female shoppers.

Ideally they would have comfortable easy chairs, free coffee and several copies of the *Telegraph* available.

> **Chris Williamson**
> Blyth, Nottinghamshire

SIR — I spend so much time waiting in the car while my wife tours the local M&S that I have decided that it would be the appropriate place, eventually, for my ashes to be scattered.

> **Alan Thomas**
> Caerphilly, Glamorgan

SIR — A year ago in New York at the cosmetics counter of Saks Fifth Avenue my husband, a man's man, hitched up onto a white leather and chrome high chair. While I was occupied with choosing facial creams, a beautiful, voluptuous assistant leant over him, flooded him with flattery, applied instant tan to his face and snipped off his Denis Healey eyebrows; he didn't make a murmur.

> **Cecilia Timmington**
> Birkdale, Lancashire

SIR — After the success of *Fifty Shades of Grey*, perhaps Marks & Spencer could reverse its fortunes by becoming S&M.

> **Sheelagh James**
> Lichfield, Staffordshire

SIR — As an independent retailer, I read with interest of Amazon's latest plans to bring their "Go" store concept to the UK High Street, where items are placed in baskets and shoppers are charged as they leave.

I think this is what we quaintly used to call "a shop".

> **Joanna Coleman**
> Shotley, Northamptonshire

SIR — When I asked where cloves might be in a nearby supermarket, the assistant suggested that I "look on the 'angers by the door."

> **Trish Page**
> Alcester, Warwickshire

# DRESSING MR AVERAGE

SIR — I have recently joined in the trend of playing walking football, and bought a new pair of trainers for the purpose. I was surprised to see printed on the box: "Average contents: two".

Presumably some poor soul will find only one trainer in the box, while Jake the Peg will be fortunate enough to get all three shoes in one purchase.

> **Michael Price**
> Ashford, Middlesex

SIR — Can any of your expert readers explain why my belt buckles move round my waist without any effort on my part — even when I have been largely sedentary?

It only occurs with corduroy trousers and can move four or five inches in a day, through the loops as well. At 83, am I a new Uri Geller?

**John H. Smith**
Cambridge

SIR — In an age of digital reminders, am I alone in still finding it useful to tie a knot in a handkerchief?

**Professor Stefan Buczacki**
Stratford-upon-Avon, Warwickshire

SIR — It is true that a relatively small number of women are forced to wear high heels or makeup at work, although many more may choose to do so. However, a much greater number of men are forced to wear jackets and ties, even in hot weather when women can wear comfortable summer frocks.

I agree that forcing women to wear high heels is ridiculous, but, surely, nothing can possibly be more sexist or demeaning than refusing to employ a man unless he comes to work wearing a leash pointing to his genitals.

**Dr Steven Field**
Wokingham, Berkshire

# BROKEN DISHWASHER

SIR — As a 62-year-old "new man", I have accepted my role as chief and only washer-upper while my wife happily kneads, cooks, bakes and so on in the kitchen.

Having just spent an hour cleaning up after her carnage I found she has found another way to break my soul. She has discovered something called chia seeds to make jam instead of pectin. These damn things stick to everything, from sponges to dish cloths to tea towels. Whoever put these things into a recipe and published it should be hung, drawn and quartered – and then made to wash up.

**John O'Neill**
Hessle, East Yorkshire

SIR – After Kirstie Allsopp's pronouncement that washing machines have no place in the kitchen how can my wife and I hold up our heads in polite society again? We have two washing machines in our kitchen.

If you've ever been hauled over the coals for washing your wife's unmentionables at the wrong temperature then let me recommend separate his and hers washing machines as a real step towards marital harmony.

**Peter Forrest**
London N5

SIR – Could readers suggest possible sentences for a husband found guilty of ramming a pair of wellingtons onto two carefully constructed chocolate roulades bound for first Christmas dinner with new "outlaws"?

**Fiona Rolt**
Blakesley, Northamptonshire

SIR – As someone who abhors housework, I have always maintained that not cleaning the windows is a sure way to avoid bird strike.

**Mary Moore**
Croydon, Surrey

# HOSEPIPE BAN

SIR – I have just had the first argument of the year with my hosepipe. Could someone please hurry up and invent a remote-control spray gun, so I can do away with the wretched thing.

**Sue Eyles**
Maidenhead, Berkshire

SIR – I would be grateful if a horticulturalist could inform me at what point the pain of weeding will blossom into the joy of gardening.

**Claire Mccombie**
Lower Ufford, Suffolk

SIR – Four years ago, I unwittingly planted a coppice in my garden with Spanish bluebells. Given a hard Brexit, will my bluebells be allowed to remain in this country?

**Dennis Wombell**
Selby, North Yorkshire

# BLOODY BREXIT!

SIR – Our home used to suffer regular mishaps – items getting broken, mud on the hall carpet and so on – and we were never sure whom to blame.

Then we acquired a dog and called it Brexit. Whatever goes wrong now we just blame the dog. If there is mud on the carpet, we blame the dog; if rain is forecast we can now blame Brexit for mud on the carpet before it has even happened.

I don't know how we managed without him.

**Peter Walton**
Buckingham

SIR – My dog Fitz has just passed away – unfortunately too early for me to get him a companion, who was to be named "Starts".

**Jane Cullinan**
Padstow, Cornwall

# PITCH AND PAT

SIR – To enliven our walks in the Yorkshire Dales, our family play a variant of Cowpat Cricket known as Jobbie Golf. It involves spearing a sheep dropping on the end of a walking pole then flinging it at an opponent as hard as possible. My eight-year-old grandson finds it highly entertaining.

**Jonathan Brocklebank**
Swynnerton, Staffordshire

SIR — In order to shame dog owners who allow their pets to mess along a local coastal walk, a friend of mine has taken to inserting little flagged cocktail sticks into the poop piles.

I hope his markers are biodegradable.

**James Logan**
Portstewart, Co Londonderry

SIR — I walk my dogs in the woods. Plastic bags of dog poo are deposited along the paths for someone to deal with. I think there is a very strong argument for the reintroduction of corporal punishment.

**Sebastian Neville-Clarke**
Vines Cross, East Sussex

# THREE GUINEAS AND A PENNY

SIR — When our youngest son was small, his beloved guinea pig died. My husband, believing that children should be told the truth about life and death, informed him that, sadly, his pet had died. Consequently, our son was devastated and cried for a week.

Some time later he grew to love his new, snowy-white guinea pig and off he went to summer camp, leaving him in our care. Unfortunately, just as the summer camp was coming to an end, Snowy died. My husband, unable to cope for a second time with the impending trauma, rushed out to buy a replacement. There were no white guinea pigs anywhere and he subsequently returned with a brown one.

On his return, our son was enthralled to learn that his guinea pig had acquired a bronze suntan after a week of excellent weather.

It would embarrass him to say how many years later it was when the penny dropped.

**Jane Parkin**
Epsom, Surrey

# BEST LEFT ON THE CUTTING-ROOM FLOOR

SIR – My daughter, now 61, confessed she had, as a pre-teen, cut out pictures of ladies in revealing lingerie from my mail-order catalogues and sold them for one penny each to boys in her class.

This is something I did not wish to know.

**Doris Grimsley**
London SE2

# BABY BOOMERANGERS

SIR – I see two big problems for home owners these days. Firstly, Japanese knotweed. The neighbours aren't too thrilled when it makes an appearance, it spreads out and rapidly takes over; it can be really expensive to deal with, and however hard you try to get rid of it, it keeps returning.

Secondly, when a grown-up child moves back home. The neighbours aren't too thrilled when it makes . . . oh, hang on.

**Jo Marchington**
Ashtead, Surrey

SIR — My parents had a plan — as soon as my sister and I had left home, they promptly moved to a flat too small for either of us to move back.

**Brian Ford**
Ashley Heath, Dorset

SIR — "Care for parents like your children", urges your headline. I am waiting for my son to phone me up and tell me he has arranged trampolining for my wife and tennis lessons for me.

**Duncan Rayner**
Sunningdale, Berkshire

# ESPRIT DE L'ESCALIER

SIR — I think there comes a point in the parenting role where you know you're getting outmanoeuvred. Round the dinner table some years back I was berating one of my teenage sons for some misdemeanour or other. Normally I would expect a feisty response. But this time there was a long pause before he replied: "What do you reckon, Dad? Is it something I inherited, or is it the way you brought me up?"

It took me two days to work out a riposte: "No, it's the company you keep."

Too little, too late, of course.

**Alan Swift**
Bristol

SIR — My daughter never listens, talks over me, and after asking a question, she interrupts constantly to demand the answer that she is in fact already getting.

She is at an age where she needs to decide what she wants to be when she grows up.

Journalism?

**Dr P.M.**
Cropredy, Oxfordshire

# DEAF SENTENCE

SIR — My wife recently went for an initial hospital appointment to check if she needed hearing aids. During the ensuing consultation, they asked my wife if she had vertigo.

"Yes," she replied, "about 20 miles away."

The aids come next week.

**Ken Tucker**
Wotton-under-Edge, Gloucestershire

SIR — When the choir I belong to sang to members of a local golf club last Christmas, among the donations received (which we collect for charity) was a battery from a hearing aid.

One can only assume the owner found it easier to remove the aid than to walk out.

**Margaret Scattergood**
Knowle, West Midlands

SIR – What is the best way to communicate with a (typically young) person who is wearing a pair of wired earpieces and apparently listening to something?

My technique is to move my lips as if silently saying something, which usually has the desired effect of the device being hastily removed.

**E.M.**
Hathersage, Derbyshire

# WHAT A BEAUTIFUL
# FIVER YOU ARE

SIR – I had been struggling to see the advantages of a plastic five pound note. However, it is reassuring to know that, should our cat (Basil) ever choose to venture to sea with an owl, his comestibles and moneys will now be well protected against the elements.

**William J. Farrant**
Bures, Suffolk

SIR – I have rapidly fallen in love with the new five pound note. Its modest size belies its sensuous, silky polymer texture and the slightly garish, yet cheeky, colourway.

I find myself resentful at having to part with them in order to purchase mere trivial goods. Do I need help?

**John O'Neill**
Hessle, East Yorkshire

SIR — Has anyone else found these new plastic fivers to be slippery customers, adept at sneaking out of your pockets?

**Doug Hoare**
Southend-on-Sea, Essex

SIR — One is annoyed that one cannot light up one's cigar with the new plastic five pound note.

**Eddie Peart**
Rotherham, South Yorkshire

SIR — I have delved into my sofas in the hope of securing a few of the reported millions of soon-to-be-obsolete pound coins.

A number of 10p and 20p coins were retrieved, along with a credit card, a comb, an earring, a toffee (in wrapper), a Christmas cracker puzzle, a walnut, a pen, two golf tees and one blue sock — but no pound coins.

**John Brough**
Maidenhead, Berkshire

SIR — I have managed to balance a new pound coin on top of another. Any attempt to do the same with a couple of one euro coins is impossible.

I know which is the more stable currency.

**Graham Bond**
Matching Green, Essex

SIR — We are told that paying cash-in-hand is "not being a good citizen". Perhaps next time I am greeted in a supermarket car park with, "Car wash, sir?" I should only

agree provided they can furnish an invoice against which
to pay.

**Terry Lloyd**
Darley Abbey, Derbyshire

# QUALITATIVE EASING

SIR – After a visit with our granddaughters to a local
wildlife park and a restaurant on the way home, we told
them that we had no money left for anything else. The
three-year-old promptly announced that we should "buy
some more money tomorrow".

Obviously a budding supporter of quantitative easing.

**Irvine Manning**
Tirley, Gloucestershire

SIR – Thirty years ago, my then six-year-old daughter
tearfully took me to task for passing by a beggar in the street
who asked me for "change for a cup of tea". I have never
turned down such a request since.

Today, in London's Victoria Street, I handed over a £1
coin, to which the gentleman of the road responded: "Tea's
£2.20 a cup round here, mate."

I summoned up a mental picture of my daughter and
paid in full.

**Charles King**
Croydon, Surrey

SIR – I have stopped lending money to friends for health reasons. It seems to affect their memories.

**Jonathan Sinclair**
London NW4

SIR – On reaching the age of 80 I have been granted an increase of 25p per week (20p after tax) to my state pension. My wife thinks that I should invest these extra funds but I am inclined to splash out on living the high life while we are still able.

What is it to be: prudence or carpe diem?

**Leonard Macauley**
Staining, Lancashire

SIR – I have just received a letter from HM Revenue & Customs informing me that I have earned £0.16 from a family trust and paid £0.04 in tax. By my crude mathematics I understand that HMRC has spent 55p in postage to tell me that I have paid them 4p.

So that's where the money goes.

**Lt Cr Ben Bosley RN (retd)**
London SE7

# THE CURSE OF KANE

SIR – Our newspaper boy is called Kane. Because of his erratic delivery service we have dubbed him Kane Unable.

**Terry Whiting**
Lincoln

SIR – I asked for three dozen second-class stamps at the sub-post office counter and the young, pleasant, well-spoken assistant said: "So that's 18 you want then?"

"No, three dozen, please."

Turning to her boss, she asked: "How many is that?" I despair.

**Geoff Neale**
Cheltenham, Gloucestershire

SIR – NS&I letters to me are addressed to Lord Penelope Laura Smith, prompting my postman to knock whenever he has one to deliver and hand it over accompanied by a low bow.

**Penny Smith**
Leigh-on-Sea, Essex

# ONCE BITTEN

SIR – While working as a postman in Wellington, New Zealand, I was the only one from my sorting office not to have been bitten on my round.

1966 found me working as a bus conductor in Birmingham, UK. While I was upstairs collecting fares, a dog got on my bus, found me upstairs and bit me on the ankle before getting off at the traffic lights. I was the only conductor in our garage to have been bitten while collecting fares.

A lot more research needs to be undertaken to prevent former postmen being bitten in later life.

**Peter Troy**
Felixstowe, Suffolk

SIR — On one occasion my normally highly tolerant and kindly grandfather finally lost his patience with a villager's Jack Russell that would always attack his ankles as he walked away from delivering their post.

Turning upon the aggressor, my grandfather took a "bend it like Beckham" swing with his right foot, but it was nimbly dodged by the intended recipient. The result was an agonising dislocated knee cartilage and lengthy period of hospitalisation.

**Stephen Stone**
Buckland in the Moor, Devon

# THE DOCTOR CAN DEFINITELY SEE YOU NOW

SIR — At hospital today I was asked to provide proof of citizenship in the form of a utility bill before being allowed to see my consultant. I really do feel that my wearing of red corduroy trousers, brogues and a tweed jacket should have been sufficient.

**Dr Bertie Dockerill**
Shildon, Co Durham

SIR — I have usually found the NHS telephone 111 service to be very good. However, I became concerned when reporting my daughter's temperature as 102 degrees and was asked by the handler: "Is that Centigrade or Fahrenheit?"

**Victor Tee**
Kintbury, Berkshire

SIR — The quality and appropriateness of hospital food is indeed lamentable. My partner, severely weakened following an emergency appendectomy, thought the "fruit salad" offered on the menu would be easy to swallow.

He was presented with an apple, an orange and a pear on a plate. He went hungry.

**Rosemary Kroiter**
Canterbury

SIR — The solution to providing an improved 24/7 NHS is very simple and incurs no cost. Rebrand NHS doctors as "veterinary surgeons" and patients as animals. Under the requirements of the Royal Veterinary College, if an animal requires treatment — whenever, and on whichever day of the week — it must be provided.

**Peter Froggatt**
Dorking, Surrey

SIR — A couple of weeks ago, following a head injury, I was taken to hospital in an ambulance bearing the registration letters PAP. When I got there I was put onto a bed with MAU (Medical Acute Unit) in large letters on the end of it.

How's that for a personalised service?

**Maureen Pappin**
Cobham, Surrey

SIR — NHS hospitals are to ban smoking on their premises, including in gardens and car parks.

Were their unfortunate patients prisoners of war, those responsible for this inhumane treatment would be in breach of Article 26 of the Geneva Convention.

**Richard Munton**
Frittenden, Kent

SIR — I recently completed the "GP Patient Survey" which runs to 62 questions, of which question 58 is: "Do you have a learning disability?"

I wonder how many people with learning disabilities can get as far as question 58.

**Bill Welland**
Somerton, Somerset

SIR — The sign in my local GP's reception offering free flu vaccination reads: "Pregnant, over 65, diabetic".

I fear that if you qualify on all three counts, you will need more than a flu injection.

**Steve Moore**
Hove, East Sussex

# HIGHBROW MINDFULNESS

SIR — I was very interested to learn about the concept of mindfulness or "living in the moment", which counsellors claim successfully combats anxiety.

I realised that I, too, have been practising mindfulness, only I have always referred to it as "plucking my eyebrows".

**Ann Goldstraw**
Tunbridge Wells, Kent

# BATTLING BT

SIR — Over the course of two months I have been passed from one BT department to another, attempting to explain the issue for the umpteenth time, to some bewildered soul on some random continent.

To illustrate BT's obsession with their own inadequate systems, I have been given the following contact references: a 20-digit order number, a 19-digit sales reference number, my 11-digit phone number and a 10-digit account number — all in addition to my name, address and postcode.

They have not yet asked for the girth of my waist or the pulsing of my headache.

**Michael Edmond**
Hoarwithy, Herefordshire

SIR — My pigeon is called 4g. Her mother was 3g and her eldest daughter is called Super Fast Broadband. They cover the whole of the UK, they're highly efficient and they're not restricted by big company politics or used as pawns by politicians.

For those interested, please leave your window open and some corn.

**James Cookson**
Morpeth, Northumberland

# MURDEROUS APPLIANCES

SIR — The Alexis voice recognition software on our Amazon Echo translated "add silver polish to my shopping list" as "add shuffle punisher to my Shopping List". I fear that adding "watch *Midsomer Murders*" to my to do list may have dire consequences.

**Debs Simcox**
Bristol

SIR – I find it difficult to understand why many hotels still put battery-powered, wall-mounted clocks in rooms. The incessant tick, tick, tick at night is extremely annoying. However, it is a superb engineering challenge in stacking odd bits of furniture in order to reach the clock and remove the batteries.

**Greg Meade**
Southampton

SIR – I have long been convinced that all hoteliers should be compelled to sleep in the rooms of their hotel at least once.

**Elisabeth Murray**
London N20

SIR – We are forever reading articles about the dangers of social media turning our children into socially redundant robots, unable to escape the clutches of these internet giants.

I myself have not yet succumbed. However, there is a lurking danger never mentioned in the press when any man undertaking a building project is online: the temptations of the Screwfix catalogue.

I have wasted hours of valuable time drooling over plumbing parts, new screw sets or that unbeatable Bosch 960SE drill.

I worry for my work, my relationships and my overall wellness.

Is there a remedy? Is Facebook the antidote?

**J.R.**
Kineton, Warwickshire

SIR – I do not wish to go into details, but if the government decides to retain my emails they will learn a great deal about septic tanks.

**L.S. Illis**
Keyhaven, Hampshire

# BREXIT BRITAIN

## LEAVE IT, DAVE

SIR – David Cameron has acquired a £25,000 shed, but he is in dispute with his children over how it should be used: a Wendy house or an author's den?

I have some advice for him – concede now. Recent history suggests you are not a good negotiator.

**P.H.**
Terling, Essex

## VOLUNTEER BREXIT NEGOTIATORS

SIR – Can it really be so difficult to sort out the rights of EU residents in the UK and their British counterparts in Europe?

Our Parish County Council is made up of "ordinary" but intelligent and informed people. I reckon that we could sort this out in a couple of hours. Throw in a glass or two of a decent red, and we could even reach an amicable solution to please everybody.

We await our summons to Brussels with great interest.

**Rev Dr Anthony Peabody**
Burghfield Common, Berkshire

SIR – May I propose that the government's Brexit Committee co-opt the services of Baldrick. At least then they will have some sort of plan, albeit a cunning one.

**John Hill**
Swansea

# DRESSING-DOWN SUNDAY

SIR – To Mrs May and her husband, photographed emerging from church dressed in jeans: God may forgive you, but I never will.

**Alison Fenton**
London W1

SIR – Since she always dresses up in local costume when visiting mosques and foreign countries, I hope Theresa May is not planning to visit a naturist beach in the near future.

**Charlotte Primrose**
Ipswich, Suffolk

SIR – I believe the Prime Minister is to be applauded for her fashion sense.

However, Ogden Nash had these words of caution:

*Sure, deck your lower limbs in pants;*
*Yours are the limbs, my sweeting.*
*You look divine as you advance—*
*Have you seen yourself retreating?*

**Doug Johnson**
Hill Head, Hampshire

SIR – Might it not be charitable to provide Philip May, the Prime Minister's husband, with a pair of braces to allow him to show that he is in total support of his wife on public appearances?

**Alexander Smith**
Worthing, West Sussex

SIR – In the interests of female equality, I permit my wife to take the bins out.

**James McNie**
Moray

# HOUSE OF COMMONERS

SIR – It may be the House of Commons, but surely not so common that Members may remove their ties?

**Crombie Glennie**
Hawksworth, Nottinghamshire

SIR – If MPs don't wear ties, how are we to tell which school, regiment or club they belong to?

**Edward Wilkinson**
Bakewell, Derbyshire

SIR – All men of a certain age need to cover their necks with something.

**Patricia Cave-Smith**
Salisbury

SIR – My neighbour has bought a "onesie" for her new grandson, printed to look like an evening suit, complete with bow tie. Could something on these lines be used to satisfy our MPs' sartorial problems?

**Ann Mott**
Southend on Sea, Essex

SIR — Samantha Cameron seems to favour sleeveless garments in her new collection.

Never mind the price of the clothes; most of us could not afford the cost of the heating bill to allow us to wear them.

**Carol A. Forshaw**
Bolton, Lancashire

## BREXIT BONNETS

SIR — I have noticed that whenever Jeremy Corbyn appears, his head and face are sheltered by one of those silly Breton fishermen's caps, suitable for Breton fishermen only. I feel something more Brexit British should adorn his nut.

May I humbly suggest that a deerstalker, with two peaks front and rear, could shelter both of his faces.

**Richard Davie**
Monmouth

## OUT AND PROUD

SIR — I do wish someone would organise a Brexit Pride march. It would appeal to at least 52 per cent of the population.

**John Naylor**
London SW20

SIR — I told my friend that, for the first time in my life, I would join a protest march to uphold the referendum vote if the Remainers thwarted Brexit. My friend (a Leaver) said that he would join as well and throw stones at me.

**B.N. Bosworth**
Blakedown, Worcestershire

SIR – I have always been in favour of a second referendum and was very pleased when David Cameron let us have it on 23 June, to enable us to correct the mistake that this country made in the first one.

**Sam Kelly**
Dobcross, Lancashire

# LORDS LEAP IN

SIR – Rather than another referendum on the EU, would it not be more productive to have one on the continued existence of the House of Lords?

**Charlotte Joseph**
Lawford, Essex

SIR – I am at a loss to understand why the Lib Dems in the House of Lords are to be provided with sleeping bags and camp beds for the long night session due to Brexit debates.

They do not normally have any trouble getting to sleep on the nice red bench seats already provided.

**Peter Thompson**
Sutton, Surrey

SIR – I stand ready and resolute to become one of the 140 new Conservative peers that the Prime Minister needs to appoint in order to have a working majority in the House of Lords.

I will resign my peerage as soon as the job is done, and that will include voting to reduce the Lords to an elected Senate of just 100 souls.

**[Lord in waiting] Mike Ostick**
Upton-upon-Severn, Worcestershire

SIR – Recent events in the UK and US reinforce the view that democracy is merely the tyranny of the majority. I have always believed that benign dictatorship is the better option – provided I can be the dictator.

**Andrew Blake**
Shalbourne, Wiltshire

# REBRANDING REMOANERS

SIR – I am fed up with being branded a Remoaner while others enjoy the swashbuckling moniker of Brexiteer. I propose a re-branding of Leavers as Brexitmongers.

**A.W.**
Northrepps, Norfolk

SIR – Brexit is so much cleverer than most Londoners realise. In addition to the numerous, very obvious – but unspecified – benefits in growth and stability, it may also solve the London housing shortage. If we can export enough financial services jobs to Frankfurt, Paris and Dublin, we will have no housing shortage at all.

**Gerald Brawn**
London SE1

SIR — I have a bet with my wife that Brexit will not happen before the new Heathrow runway is built. If nothing else, at least the government has given us something to talk about at breakfast for the next decade.

**Sacha Tomes**
Rudford, Gloucestershire

# A KIP FOR UKIP

SIR — Given that UKIP has achieved "I" for the "UK", surely there is now no need for the "P"?

**James Close-Smith**
Stowe, Buckinghamshire

SIR — Is it not time that UKIP got itself a grown-up logo? The "pound shop" image was valid when keeping sterling was the principal issue.

**Tim Lovett**
Claygate, Surrey

SIR — Not only is the Conservative government setting about implementing UKIP's core policy, they are now preparing to introduce more grammar schools — another UKIP 2015 manifesto policy.

However, UKIP still has some way to go until they have as many policies adopted by the government as the Monster Raving Loony Party achieved.

**Malcolm Warburton**
Sandbach, Cheshire

# ELEVEN MINUS

SIR – I would hazard a guess that the vast majority of people who, like Theresa May, so keenly support grammar schools are those who are convinced that they (and their children) are clever enough to pass the exam.

Should they discover themselves to be in that much larger group of individuals who messed up on the day, weren't tutored sufficiently or, heaven forbid, just weren't quite clever enough to get a place, I imagine their support might wane.

**Emma Jackson**
Henley-on-Thames, Oxfordshire

SIR – As a professional I often acted for a much wealthier former schoolmate. He had left school at 15, taken an apprenticeship and became a prosperous plumber.

Whenever the topic of wealth arose he would comment: "You know your mistake, you passed your 11 plus."

**Terence M. Bailey**
Little Oakley, Northamptonshire

SIR – Thank God prison league tables are being dropped. I had enough trouble trying to get the kids into decent schools.

**Peter Sharp**
Ascot, Berkshire

# PARLIAMENTARY QUESTION TIME

SIR – Assume that there was a mistake in redrawing the boundaries and you lost your MP entirely. How long would it be before you noticed, if ever?

**Denis Kearney**
Lostwithiel, Cornwall

# FIELDS OF MAY

SIR – Have Piers Morgan or Michael Gove ever run through a wheat field, as Mrs May claims to have done?

Having lived on a farm in Suffolk for a long time, I have never seen anyone do this. Try it. You will find the experience quite painful, the ground uneven and the wheat stalks scratchy.

Good luck!

**Gill Harris**
Sudbury, Suffolk

SIR – As Theresa May has admitted she is terrified of snakes, will she be able to bring herself to enter the Cobra room?

**J.F. Bailey**
Henley-on-Thames, Oxfordshire

# A TALE OF ONE CITY

SIR – As we agonise over the desire to preserve the liberties of Parliament while accepting the need for greater security, it is interesting that as early as 1841, when Charles Dickens published *Barnaby Rudge*, his novel charting the 1780 Gordon Riots in London, the vulnerability of Parliament was noted:

"They went slowly down to Westminster, where both Houses of Parliament were sitting. Mingling in the crowd, they lounged about; while Hugh's new friend pointed out to him significantly the weak parts of the building, how easy it was to get into the lobby, and so to the very door of the House of Commons". (Chapter XXXVIII)

**Simon Eliot**
Bath

SIR — I was delighted to read that Cressida Dick would like "diversity" to be at the heart of her tenure as Metropolitan Police Commissioner. How refreshing for the residents of Greater London to know that she has moved on from such passé trivia as catching criminals and locking them up.

**Paul Goodson**
Plaxtol, Kent

# NO MOTHER THERESA

SIR — The fuss over the Prime Minister with regards to the Grenfell tragedy is absurd — and no doubt stoked by Leftist agitators. It is not the Prime Minister's job to comfort, but to run the country. While no politician dare say it, as cheap populism is in the ascendant, emollience is not their business, but that of the clergy.

**Fr Marcus P.M. Stewart**
Broadstairs, Kent

SIR — It is becoming plainer by the day that Mrs May is suffering from a chronic condition which afflicts many adults born before the millennial generation.

Its symptoms are an inability to emote to order in public and a refusal to make spontaneous physical contact with others with cameras present. It is a disorder which won us two world wars.

Pre-Diana era, sobbing to order was anathema to members of the House of Windsor.

Mrs May has faced three major terror attacks and the worst civilian disaster in decades, yet she has not dissolved into a weeping, touchy-feely mess on TV.

She must be forgiven; that was once called the mark of leadership.

**Anthony Rodriguez**
Staines-upon-Thames, Middlesex

SIR — I am becoming increasingly concerned that Jeremy Corbyn will seriously injure himself as he attempts to leap onto every passing bandwagon.

**Michael Amies**
Pershore, Worcestershire

SIR — One of the memories I will have of the various recent disasters is of television reporters asking victims and their families how they feel.

**Q. David McGill**
Sutton Coldfield, West Midlands

# HOW THE WEST WAS WON

SIR — Tim Bowles's splendid election victory makes him the "Mayor of the West of England Metropolitan Area". May I suggest that this lengthy and slightly clumsy title might be shortened in everyday usage to "Western Super-Mayor"?

**Dr Richard Austen-Baker**
Abbeystead, Lancashire

# I'M SORRY, SHE HASN'T A CLUE

SIR — The nine-letter solution to the Polyword puzzle on 18 April was "Candidate". This was published on the day that Mrs May called a snap general election.

Does the *Telegraph* have sources of information we should be told about?

**Steve Howe**
East Tilbury, Essex

SIR — Who would have guessed that Mrs May was a talented magician? With the words "general election", the rest of the world seems to have disappeared.

**Margie Haynes**
Colchester, Essex

SIR — "Strong and stable" is the Conservative Party's election mantra. I had a tree stump in my front garden like that.

**Richard Phillips**
Newbury, Berkshire

SIR – The new game in our home is to get the words "strong and stable" into the conversation.

This morning I had a shower and the flow of water was disrupted by the filling of the washing machine: not a strong and stable water flow. I also hoped my husband had pegged out the washing in a strong and stable fashion in order that it didn't blow away in the wind.

**Elaine Caffrey**
Halifax

SIR – I note that the stylised bird on the Liberal Democrats logo has asymmetric wings. This means that it can only fly in circles. Says it all, really.

**Christopher Newns**
Knowle, West Midlands

SIR – My grandson asked me: "What would you do if the Conservatives lost the June election, if a new left-wing coalition decided to stay in the EU and the Scots voted for independence in a second referendum?"

"Shoot myself," I replied.

**George K. McMillan**
Perth

# ICE CREAM TOMORROW

SIR – As a young lad in the days just before the war, I recall the teacher introducing the subject of voting and elections. To illustrate his lesson he selected five boys, of whom I was one, to stand as candidates and compose an address to persuade the class to vote for him.

The main point of the boy who won was to promise that if he was elected he could arrange for all boys to get unlimited free ice creams at the local Woolworths.

**Dan Godfrey**
Caerphilly, Glamorgan

SIR – I do wonder, as an encouragement to vote, whether the younger generation should be offered a free glass of Prosecco with every ballot paper. It seems to be the usual offer on everything these days.

**Andrew Bolton**
Nottingham

SIR – The party that guarantees to curtail the issue of catchpenny commemorative stamps, and requires postmen to wear proper trousers instead of those ridiculous shorts, will get my vote.

**John Carter**
Bromley, Kent

SIR – The Green Party have proposed a four-day working week. Whether we finish the week on a Thursday, or even Wednesday, I am sure that we will keep our inalienable right to knock off a bit early on the last afternoon.

**Bruce Cochrane**
Bridge of Allan, Stirling

SIR – While attempting to arrange a lift to the polling station, I was somewhat discomfited when the Greens' candidate told me to walk or use a bicycle. Although I did

not vote for them, the Tories were kind enough to send me
something satisfyingly large, noisy and polluting.

**John Eoin Douglas**
Edinburgh

SIR – Not a single candidate has called on us this campaign.
Only one leaflet has been delivered (from Labour). We
did sight two official-looking people with identity tags and
clipboards lurking in our vicinity but the knock on the door
five minutes later was from a glazing company.

Our conclusion? We are going for a new conservatory.

**David Leech**
Balcombe, West Sussex

SIR – A local election candidate did actually call for a
chat on my doorstep. Keen, however, to get back to my
breakfast, I interrupted him with the assurance: "Don't
worry, you're with friends here."

Only afterwards did I realise that my flies were wide
open.

**Peter Wellington**
Marlow, Buckinghamshire

SIR – There must have been something wrong with the
voting paper I received at the polling station, for it did
not include the names of either Theresa May or Jeremy
Corbyn. Throughout the electioneering we were being told
to vote for them in person, but how could we do so if their
names were not on the ballot?

**Miles Williamson-Noble**
Pickworth, Lincolnshire

SIR — To save paper, should we keep the election leaflets from this last election ready for the next?

**Michael Robinson**
Chillerton, Isle of Wight

SIR — With the current confusion surrounding the policies of the political parties and the rather restricted choice for our imminent future leader, might Mr Obama be able to quickly make himself available as an alternative?

**Lindsay Cressey**
Newcastle upon Tyne

SIR — For half a century, I have been an enthusiastic participant in voting at general elections.

The latest round of political bungling and posturing has turned me off the whole process.

The only thing which would tempt me back to the ballot box now would be if Joanna Lumley stepped up and offered to lead our country out of this ghastly mess.

**James L. Shearer**
Edinburgh

# ROLLING MONEY TREES

SIR — It appears that the Labour Party is proposing a "rolling manifesto". Otherwise known as: "Making it up as you go along".

**Michael Bacon**
Bordon, Hampshire

SIR – Let's be fair to Labour: there's enough fertiliser in their manifesto for a large forest of money trees.

**R.A. Underwood**
Newcastle upon Tyne

SIR – How can anyone doubt Labour's manifesto, when a similar one has been so successful in Greece?

**Peter Iden**
Totnes, Devon

SIR – I could see only one thing wrong with Labour's draft manifesto: the silent "R". I wonder if this defect will be corrected in the final version?

**Jon Bell**
Staple Fitzpaine, Somerset

SIR – What is it that the Labour Party and Jeremy Corbyn have against "The Few"?

After all, they did a good job at Agincourt and the Battle of Britain.

**Mark Baker**
Tenterden, Kent

SIR – What fallback plan do Labour have to recoup the tax take should the top 5 per cent of earners decide to decline "the invitation to pay a little more"?

**Major Keith Miles (retd)**
Hythe, Kent

SIR – Is it just a coincidence that Jeremy Corbyn thinks that anyone earning over £80,000 is rich, while an MP's salary is £74,962?

**Michael Glover**
Dinton, Wiltshire

SIR – It is quite possible that, after the general election, the Labour Party will split and will have to rebrand itself.

May I propose that the faction led by Mr Corbyn and Mr McDonnell be renamed Marx and Spender.

**Glenn Viney**
Maidenhead, Berkshire

SIR – I am somewhat bemused by the thought of an avowed Marxist proposing workers' holidays to celebrate religious feast days. Has he no principles?

**Hugh Emerson**
Wistaston, Cheshire

SIR – Why on earth would Jeremy Corbyn think that offering us more Bank Holidays, when the weather is traditionally awful, might help Labour win the forthcoming general election?

We have quite enough wet, cold and miserable weekends during the year without him foisting another four on us.

**Charles Garth**
Ampthill, Bedfordshire

SIR – We are all accustomed to pre-election sweeteners but after Jeremy Corbyn presented a jar of his home-made jam live to the cast of *The One Show*, I am intrigued as to what other delicacies are on offer.

**Russell Edwards**
Beckley, East Sussex

SIR – As I understand it, at least one of Mr Corbyn's children was sent "against his will" to a selective school. Presumably Mr Corbyn must have entered into negotiations with the child's mother on the subject, and lost out in those negotiations.

He now asks us to vote for him as Prime Minister, and to put him in a position to negotiate with the EU about the country's future.

**Bernard Ideson**
Cowling, West Yorkshire

## TRUE TERROR

SIR – What is terror? It is the feeling that comes over me when I consider the possibility of Diane Abbott being in charge of our counter-terrorism strategy.

**Keith J. Vaughan**
Great Stretton, Leicestershire

SIR – Has Diane Abbott learnt nothing from Emily Thornberry on what to do when you are asked something by a journalist, but you had dozed through the briefing?

(i) Accuse the questioner of sexism.
(ii) Dismiss the question as a pub quiz.
(iii) Sit back, wearing a smug expression.

**Ernie Waddell**
Edlesborough, Buckinghamshire

SIR — If the Tories want to achieve reduced net migration, the obvious solution is to let Diane Abbott do the calculations.

**Fred Wilson**
Newcastle upon Tyne

# MOBILISING THE GREY VOTE

SIR — I discovered, by chance, that one of my long deceased neighbours is on the 2017 electoral roll.

So I notified the local electoral services office, as this might imply a case of electoral fraud. The officer to whom I spoke said: "He didn't notify us he died. So he remained on the roll."

It seems, therefore, that Theresa May is missing a trick. There's nothing in the Conservative manifesto for dead voters. There may be a significant number of them. Her party could offer "Get out of Hell free" cards for individuals who have clearly repented. Bigger war memorials. Underground Wi-Fi in graveyards.

I feel sure these policies would appeal.

**Danny Connolley**
London WC1

# CONSERVATIVE TEARS

SIR – I don't think Theresa May was the only one to shed a little tear at the result of the election exit poll.

> **Paul McCaffrey**
> London NW5

SIR – A sad incident occurred this evening which reminded me of the general election result.

A fly flew into my iced milkshake and in the process died of the cold. I claimed victory in that my enemy died a cold, hard death without flying off into the distance. Yet I then found myself in an equally losing position of not being able to drink my milkshake.

Perhaps I should call for another milkshake?

> **James Thompson**
> Croydon, Surrey

SIR – Young versus old, Marxists versus Conservatives, austerity versus extravagance and Remainers versus Brexiteers. Oh, and a Tory party with a lame duck leader, and a Labour party apparently about to split in two.

My, my, what a merry little country we will be for the next few years.

> **Chris Nancollas**
> Yorkley, Gloucestershire

SIR – Buy gold, tinned food, bottled water, hunker down. Disgruntled.

> **Hugh Lantos**
> Litton Cheney, Dorset

SIR – I suggest we dust off the well-documented plan of the 1960s to have a military coup with the Duke of Edinburgh as head of state.

**Dorian Wood**
Clanville, Somerset

SIR – Come Friday morning I was so energised by the Tory humiliation that I managed a balancing position at my Pilates class considered to be unachievable for a woman of my age.

**Julie Grundy**
Ramsbottom, Lancashire

SIR – The suffix "ster" usually denotes someone to avoid: fraudster, gangster, mobster. Is that perhaps why people have failed to divulge their true intentions to the pollster?

**Maggie Lane Jameson**
Exeter

SIR – I think the experts who carry out polls attract undue criticism. I always find them remarkably reliable. One simply listens to their predictions and the opposite is invariably correct.

**Mark Stephens**
Hungerford, Berkshire

SIR – I do hope that whoever masterminded the Conservative campaign in the election has nothing to do with the Brexit negotiations. We can well do without another resounding success like that.

**Charles Penfold**
Ulverston, Cumbria

SIR – Will Sir Lynton Crosby give his knighthood back?

**Dr John Doherty**
Stratford-upon-Avon, Warwickshire

SIR – The Conservatives were facing open goals in every direction. Their response was to kick the ball into the stands where it hit their supporters in the face. The result is not a surprise.

**Christopher Thompson**
Ross-on-Wye, Herefordshire

SIR – Does the repeated chiming of Big Ben affect the hearing of our politicians?

After each election there is, invariably, a group of them claiming that they should have listened more carefully to the electorate.

**Christopher Hartley**
London SE25

SIR – Mrs May was right: voting for Corbyn's Labour Party was a recipe for a Coalition of Chaos. But did she have to go to such lengths to prove the point?

**John Bushby**
Marlow, Buckinghamshire

# DEAD WOMAN WALKING

SIR – Mrs May's ill-considered decision to call a snap election merely underlines my deep-seated scepticism of the merits of hiking.

> **Stephen Wallis**
> Billericay, Essex

SIR – I glad I'm not in (any of) Mrs May's shoes.

> **Colin Cummings**
> Yelvertoft, Northamptonshire

SIR – Margaret Thatcher reminded the young that no one would have remembered the Good Samaritan unless he'd had some money.

Jeremy Corbyn has convinced the young that he can be a Good Samaritan with other people's money.

Theresa May has convinced the electorate that she needs to call the Samaritans.

> **Andrew McNeilis**
> London E3

SIR – In declaring that at least she "had the balls to call an election", Mrs May seems to have forgotten that Mrs Thatcher also said that "every Prime Minister needs a Willie".

Mrs May certainly seems to have been deficient in that department.

> **Terry Bannister**
> London N20

SIR — Since Mrs May "had the balls to call the election", it is perhaps fitting that she should now end up with a well-hung Parliament.

**Alan Linfield**
Tring, Hertfordshire

SIR — I am a keen sunbather and looking forward to taking my shirt off as soon as possible. I always listened to my grandparents' advice and followed the old adage, "Ne'er cast a clout til May is out".

Can anyone tell me how long I will have to wait?

**Peter F. Baines**
Sale, Cheshire

# THE SMACK OF FIRM GOVERNMENT

SIR — I am fully in support of Jacob Rees-Mogg taking over the reins of power, with the proviso that Nanny must be a member of cabinet.

**Keith White**
Wylye, Wiltshire

SIR — There is only one obvious hair apparent. It's got to be Boris.

**Norman Fox**
Needham Market, Suffolk

SIR — Should Larry the Downing Street cat be in the running for new Tory leader?

**Susan Lyon-Heap**
Aston juxta Mondrum, Cheshire

# PIED PIPER OF ISLINGTON

SIR — With so many younger people apparently willing to entrust Jeremy Corbyn to run the country, doesn't this put into sharp focus the chronic decline in educational standards?

**David Howse**
Barton, Cambridgeshire

SIR — This, the same week it was reported that 20 per cent of British youngsters think fish fingers are made from chicken.

**A.L.**
Newcastle upon Tyne

SIR — What young person would not vote for a political party that offered them a free pub crawl for three or so years?

**Geoff Johnson**
Gateshead, Tyne and Wear

SIR — Those young voters who voted Labour because they believed Jeremy Corbyn when he promised all things to everybody are probably regretting it now that it has been revealed that he can't even do a high-five.

**Colin Bridger**
Frimley, Surrey

SIR — Jeremy Corbyn should beware quoting Shelley to the adoring Glastonbury masses. He should heed the fate of the Roman Cicero, the last politician who combined great literature and public office.

His meddling failed, he was forced to flee and he had his head and right hand chopped off and displayed in public. The tongue that inspired the crowds met a similarly gruesome fate — jabbed with pins to punish him for his anti-government prose.

No wonder Boris is lying low and avoiding random quotes from Ovid, for the moment.

**Anthony Rodriguez**
Staines-upon-Thames, Middlesex

SIR — When Jeremy Corbyn was barnstorming at Glastonbury, he was addressing the "masses" who each paid more for their tickets than the "elite" at Glyndebourne.

**Maxim Segal**
London N3

SIR — Have we left it too late? Whenever I am in town I keep meeting Jeremy Corbyn clones.

**John Francklow**
Ludlow, Shropshire

SIR — Given the dwindling pool of candidates for the Labour Party's front bench, I am available for selection. I don't agree with Mr Corbyn, which appears to make me an ideal choice.

**Anne Jappie**
Cheltenham, Gloucestershire

SIR — I trust that those Conservatives who, purely out of mischief, temporarily became Labour "supporters" to endorse Jeremy Corbyn's bid for the party leadership are reflecting on their folly in bringing the nation to the brink.

**Dr Millan Sachania**
Chertsey, Surrey

SIR — I bought a lottery ticket yesterday, hoping to win £85 million. I didn't win. But in the true spirit of Jeremy Corbyn, I'm going to say I won loudly and often, and wait for the lottery to pay up.

**Nicola Saunders**
Shalfleet, Isle of Wight

SIR — The fact that Jeremy Corbyn believes Labour to have won the election, despite gaining fewer votes and winning fewer seats than the Conservatives, tells you all you need to know about why he should never be in charge of the economy.

**David Jordan**
Broad Town, Wiltshire

SIR — If Jeremy Corbyn were being interviewed as the Captain of the *Titanic* following its tragic loss, he would say that he was "a bit disappointed but we had an excellent dinner beforehand, the band never sounded better and the crew were all Union members".

**K.R. Carhart**
Ripon, North Yorkshire

# THE LONGER SULK

SIR — As George Osborne is younger than Ted Heath, he may break his record for the longest sulk in political history.

**Mike Lewington**
London SE26

SIR — In the spirit of George Osborne's appointment as the new Editor of the *Evening Standard*, I'd like to make an early pitch to replace Mark Carney as Governor of the Bank of England when the post becomes vacant in 2019.

I have a Maths O level (Grade 6, resit, 1973), a bank account and an ISA. I do hope this won't make me overqualified for the post.

**Lynne Carlisle**
Coal Aston, Derbyshire

SIR — George Osborne says that the people need authoritative facts. After his last offering of authoritative facts regarding the doom-laden forecast for Brexit, I don't think anyone believes he is credible.

Good job the *Evening Standard* is a free paper.

**Janet Milliken**
Capel-le-Ferne, Kent

SIR — Perhaps Mr Osborne should have pasted on his mirror, into which he no doubt gazes constantly, the following quotation from Juvenal: "Revenge is always the weak pleasure of a little and narrow mind."

**Ian Wilson**
Shoreham-by-Sea, West Sussex

SIR — If George Osborne showed me a whelk and told me it was a whelk, I would not believe him.

**P.M.**
Long Sutton, Lincolnshire

SIR — In one way things improved under the Conservatives. In his last Budget speech, George Osborne still included the inevitable rise in the duty of beer but at least he said that it would add "one penny", instead of "one pence", to the price of a pint.

**Simon J. Gleaden**
Retford, Nottinghamshire

# HAMMOND IN HOT WATER

SIR — There are different levels of loyalty. There is outside, pissing in — and inside, pissing out. Mr Hammond is inside, pissing in.

**Peter Fines**
Ticknall, Derbyshire

SIR — It's all very well for modern politicians to say that people are "weary" of austerity (or as any sensible person would say, living within our means).

What if we British had said in 1940 or 1941 that we were "tired of war"? Where would we be now?

**Simon Watson**
Romsey, Hampshire

SIR – A few paving slabs in the local shopping precinct needed relaying. Five men arrived, all wearing hard hats and hi-vis jackets. Four of them did a lot of pointing and looking up at the sky, presumably in an attempt to forecast the weather. Only one was using the solitary spade they had collectively brought along.

No wonder UK productivity is so bad.

**John Newman**
Hinckley, Leicestershire

# STURGEON FLOUNDERING

SIR – In the International Maritime Code the Scottish flag means: "My vessel is stopped and making no way through the water."

Should Nicola Sturgeon consider changing the flag or its meaning before trying to change the status of the nation?

**George Watson**
Sudbourne, Suffolk

SIR – Being a more mature sort of chap, I have a thing for bossy women. My dream date would be a candlelit dinner with Nicola Sturgeon.

Over a glass of Champagne I would hold those small but powerful hands, stare dreamily into those flinty eyes and ask her the one question that burns in every Englishman's heart: "Why do you hate us so much?"

**Michael Evans**
Buckhurst Hill, Essex

SIR — We are told that Nicola Sturgeon has been obsessed with the idea of Scottish independence since the age of 15. When I was 15, I was "in love" with Trevor Howard, even though he was old enough to be my father. I watched all his films over and over again.

Then I grew up.

**G.L.**
Westgate-on-Sea, Kent

SIR — Perhaps Ms Sturgeon could be crowned Empress of Rockall, the 25-metre-wide island off the west coast of mainland Scotland. Ruling independently over both her supporters, and sustained by a couple of haggis trees, surely her lust for power would be satisfied?

More importantly, it would keep her off the front page of the *Telegraph* for a while.

**Gwynne Owen-Smith**
Kennington, Kent

SIR — I turn the sound off on my television every time Nicola Sturgeon appears. Does this save electricity?

**Sheila Culver**
Hook, Hampshire

SIR — In 2014 the separatists asked for a Yes vote and were thereby able to portray themselves as progressive — not bad for a movement that wishes to turn the clock back 300 years.

The question this time should be: "Do you wish Scotland to remain in the United Kingdom?" That should be worth at least 10 percentage points at the outset — and cause mass inconvenience for the Nats when they have to change their car stickers.

> **Donald W. Macdonald**
> Kirkcudbright, Galloway

SIR — If, as the SNP would have us believe, Britain's opting to leave the European Union is akin to shooting oneself in the foot, then surely Scotland opting to leave the UK after Brexit is akin to shooting yourself in the remaining foot and then kneecapping yourself for good measure?

> **Peter Douglas**
> Hexham, Northumberland

SIR — Bankruptcy would surely enable Scotland to be granted immediate entry into the European Union, as this seems to be a requirement.

> **Gerald Huxley**
> Bramhall, Cheshire

SIR — I have often been told by Scots that "many a mickle makes a muckle", but none can ever tell me how many mickles comprise a muckle. This seems to be a very basic concept to quantify if they leave both the Union and the EU and have to adopt it as their national currency.

**Mark Robbins**
Bruton, Somerset

# BRUSSELS POUTS

SIR — Jean-Claude Juncker apparently said the "EU is not a golf club" that members can leave at any time.

Indeed, it is not. It's much more like the Mafia, which you can join — at a high price — but if you want to leave, they will try to kill you.

**Nick Farmer**
Leicester

SIR — Should *Ode to Joy* be replaced by the theme tune to *The Godfather*?

**Chris Davies**
Ottershaw, Surrey

SIR — The behaviour of EU leaders reminds me of the moment in *The Shawshank Redemption* when the warder realises that Andy has escaped.

**C.P.**
London SW10

SIR — Is the EU the European Union or the Extortion Union?

**Tom Fairbrother**
Oxford

SIR – In the period from 1969 to when we joined the EEC in 1973 I often read in these columns how our European friends were looking forward to learning our traditional diplomatic skills.

Recent events show us that they have learnt precious little.

**Julian Phillips**
Manchester

SIR – I have several 50 pence pieces dated 1973 featuring a circle of hands, minted to celebrate the United Kingdom's accession to what was originally called the European Economic Community.

The Royal Mint website states that this 1973 coin "symbolises the nine members of the Community, clasping one another in a mutual gesture of trust, assistance and friendship." That didn't last long, did it?

**Alan Winstanley**
Ulceby, Lincolnshire

SIR – We should all be grateful to Mr Juncker. In one visit he has managed to convert previously reluctant Remainers to committed Leavers.

**Mike Patterson**
Camberley, Surrey

SIR – I gather that Donald Tusk has warned us that there "won't be any cake on the table – only salt and vinegar". Doesn't he know that that's our favourite – especially on our fish and chips?

Oh, and we'll be getting our fishing grounds back too.

**Christopher Monniot**
Rodley, West Yorkshire

SIR — Now that Messrs Juncker and Tusk have taken up the roles of stereotypical Anglophobic "Johnny Foreigners", I have taken to using their names as all-purpose ersatz swear words.

For example: "I say, the driver of that white van is a tusking juncker."

I have yet to find an opportunity for which these are not appropriate and rather satisfying.

**Hugh Neve**
Littlehampton, West Sussex

SIR — I suggest our Armed Forces take over the European Parliament and replace the despotic unelected commissioners with our own. The remaining 27 members would take at least a decade to decide where to build a new parliament building — and another decade or two to raise a unified army to oust us.

Not only would the financing of this invasion be much less than our painful Brexit settlement, it would also allow us to enjoy an uninterrupted summer of cricket.

**Mark Langdon**
Perranporth, Cornwall

SIR — Would blowing up the Channel Tunnel constitute a "hard" Brexit?

**Peter John**
Goodwick, Pembrokeshire

# PAYING FOR THE END OF THE AFFAIR

SIR — If we do end up having to pay into the EU coffers for tariff-free access, please let's label it as "foreign aid".

**Philip Valori**
London EC2

SIR — We should certainly settle honourably any genuine obligations to the EU. I suggest we employ the Brussels system of accounting and the French speed and procedure for such payments.

**Hugh Davy**
Thames Ditton, Surrey

SIR — As we still run an annual budget deficit, any sum we may have to pay the EU as a departure penalty will have to be borrowed from somewhere. Surely the sensible thing to do would be to borrow the sum from the European Central Bank before we leave and then pay it to the EU as our settlement?

This could be termed a "Greek solution".

**Nigel Dyson**
West Worldham, Hampshire

SIR — I am waiting for the EU to demand that we give Cornwall to France.

**Charlotte Joseph**
Lawford, Essex

SIR – The EU wishes to define the terms for the UK's "divorce" from the EU. I believe that the usual settlement is to split assets on a 50:50 basis.

Perhaps the EU could take Northern Ireland for a pizza every other weekend.

**Hugh Neve**
Littlehampton, West Sussex

SIR – The description of the UK leaving the EU as a divorce is ridiculous. Marriage to 27 countries is polygamy gone mad. There was no marriage; there can be no divorce.

It is better to say that the UK entered a community which it wishes to leave by a release of vows. We no longer share its ethos and self-understanding. We brought a dowry with us, the fisheries, a £200 million joining fee and much else besides.

**Rev Dr Edward Bundock**
West Raynham, Norfolk

SIR – Wolfgang Schäuble is keeping the marital bed warm, hoping we'll change our mind. Soon, it'll be sexy underwear and our favourite dinner on offer. It's a neat deflection from Germany's rule-breaking current account surplus and exploitation of the common currency. For the sake of the rest, it is Germany which should leave the EU.

**Vivian Bush**
Hessle, East Yorkshire

SIR – I find the timelines for the Brexit process, published online, most helpful.

Could you now give a date at which, in the words of Noël Coward, we can start being "beastly to the Germans".

**S.D.**
Harrow, Middlesex

SIR – I want to give up my gym membership. I have to trigger Article 666 and negotiate my departure over two to ten years.

Naturally I want to keep paying the fees to have access to the snack machine, but I will not expect anything else as I do not want to offend the management and I am a complete fool.

**Charlotte Joseph**
Lawford, Essex

SIR – To paraphrase Groucho Marx, I don't want to belong to any club that won't let me resign my membership.

**H. Porter**
Twickenham, Middlesex

SIR – I have a simple solution as to what should happen to Gibraltar – we should sell it to the EU. I would think £100 billion would just about cover it. Those living there are generally pro-Remain and those working there often reside in Spain, so what's not to like?

**David Bailey**
Burgess Hill, West Sussex

SIR – I've an idea. If the European Union is a failure, why don't we just agree to trade together? We could call it a "Common Market".

**John Weller**
North Tawton, Devon

SIR – When Brexit is complete, do you think we could have 240 pennies back in the pound? You could do such a lot with them.

**Carole Cronin**
Chelmsford, Essex

# OSTRACISING TONY

SIR – The constant attempts by Tony Blair to undermine the public make me wish that we had that further safeguard of democracy that its ancient Athenian inventors enjoyed, namely ostracism, whereby the people wrote the name of a suspect politician on a potsherd (ostrakon) and put it in an urn, the name with the most votes being then banished from the state for ten years.

Today we could do it electronically of course, and how satisfying it would be to get rid of Blair for a whole decade.

It might also concentrate Sir John Major's mind, as he would otherwise be a prime candidate for the next round.

**Dr Peter Greenhalgh**
Lyminge, Kent

SIR – If there cannot be a statue to Lady Thatcher in Parliament Square, then I suggest its replacement: a statue to Mr Blair.

If the sculpture were to depict him sat in the stocks in medieval fashion, then who could possibly be offended?

**M. Colley**
Peterborough, Cambridgeshire

SIR – We should all encourage Tony Blair to actively pursue his desire to take part in the forthcoming general elections by standing again as an MP. In fact, we ought to petition him to do so. At long last this will give the electorate the opportunity we have all yearned for, which is to relegate him to the dustbin of political history once and for all.

**Jean Maigrot**
Wortham, Norfolk

SIR – If Tony Blair makes a political comeback, won't we have to have Gordon Brown too?

**G.C.**
London SW13

SIR – Whatever the problem may be, the solution is not, nor will it ever be, Tony Blair.

**W.W.**
London SW11

SIR – Mr Blair tells us it's "hard to be hated" for taking us into the Iraq War.

Please reassure him there were lots of other things we hated him for, not just the Iraq War.

**Ginny Martin**
Bishops Waltham, Hampshire

SIR – Why does Tony Blair persist in pronouncing "Brexit" as "Breggzit"? Surely (or "shoo-erly", as he would say) the letter "x" in the English language should sound like "eks" and not "eggs".

Perhaps he pronounces "sex" as "seggs".

**Alan Paul**
London SW19

# THE USE AND
# ABUSE OF
# LANGUAGE

# THE WINDS OF CHANGE

SIR – I note that, in conversation with her husband, Samantha Cameron, the wife of our most recent ex-Prime Minister, addresses him as "babe". The winds of change are, indeed, howling more forcefully than I had previously realised.

**David Salter**
Kew, Surrrey

SIR – My quest to stop my daughters starting a sentence, or indeed a whole conversation, with the word "so" has not been helped by Theresa May choosing to do just this.

Can she assure us that her new grammar schools will teach conventional grammar?

**Alasdair Ogilvy**
Stedham, West Sussex

# JUST A POSITION

SIR – A lengthy email was sent recently by the Literacy Co-ordinator at my grandson's primary school. It described the school's spelling policy and the ways in which parents and carers could help their children with spelling.

Apart from several missing commas and the misuse of practice/practise, the Co-ordinator had written "as a pose to", instead of "as opposed to".

Is there any hope?

**Joanna Wakefield**
Danbury, Essex

# THINK BEFORE YOU INK

SIR – Many years ago my Spanish friend was asked to tattoo "Hells Angels" on a large, potentially aggressive biker. The resulting "Hells Angles" tattoo on his arm was not appreciated.

**M. Sasiadek**
London SE18

SIR – As a casualty officer in Chichester in the mid-1980s, I was faced with suturing the forearm of a young man who had been attacked with a knife. The cut went straight through a tattoo of a girl's name. When I apologised that I might not be able to align the letters properly, he replied: "Don't worry – she was a slag."

**Dr David Bennett**
Field Dalling, Norfolk

# FUNDING THE, LIKE, NHS?

SIR – The financial problems facing the NHS might be resolved by imposing a fine on those who overuse the word "like" or favour the upward inflexion to turn every remark into a question.

Levied at 1p per misdemeanour, the NHS funding crisis would be resolved in a week.

**Eldon Sandys**
Pyrford, Surrey

SIR — I was sorry to hear the Vice President of the Royal College of Surgeons refer, on the radio, to patients having "surgeries". In my day patients had operations.

Presumably this change has been influenced by the American medical soap. I blame George Clooney.

**Martin Thomas FRCS**
Bosham, West Sussex

SIR — We have been taught for some years now to use the word *issue* — and more latterly *challenge* — instead of *problem*, presumably promoted by the notion that the replacement words were less frightening and brought to the user a comfortable feeling that the matter concerned was more capable of solution.

The net result is that whenever I hear the word *problem*, I start to shake and reach for my tablets.

**Nick Trevor**
London SW4

SIR — In 2010 I attended a large meeting of healthcare professionals on the topic of management.

I made the following note: "Obviously e-CBH should work in an intermeshed transitional relationship with incentivised L-GPNT clusters to fully and transparently achieve pre-planned nationally agreed centile related target points".

Free translations into Klingon are available on request.

**Dr P.E.P.**
Coleshill, Warwickshire

SIR — I visited my dentist today to learn that I no longer have teeth, but units.

**Jim Vantassel**
Shottermill, Surrey

SIR — I am regularly called *love, dear, darling* and even *gorgeous* by the nurses who are keeping me alive at my dialysis unit.

At nearly 90 years of age, I love it.

**D.T.**
Crewe, Cheshire

# HOW DO YOU SAY LOCH IN ENGLISH?

SIR — While on the train between Inverness and the Kyle back in the late 1990s, as we passed Loch Garve, early in the journey, an American at the next table asked whether *loch* was Scottish for *lake*.

The Scotsman replied that in fact *lake* was the English for *loch*.

No doubt where his vote lies, then.

**Richard Dean**
Wymondham, Norfolk

SIR — In the 1950s, the sides of railway bridges crossing the main roads in Glasgow used to be adorned with "Down with the Pope". I was assured by a local that this was because there wasn't room to write "Down with the Moderator of the General Assembly of the Church of Scotland".

**David Sillar**
Crinan, Argyll

SIR — I have just seen "free-range scotch eggs" advertised in the window of a deli.

**B.C. Thomas**
Sellicks Green, Somerset

# REPEAT OFFENDER

SIR — When my father orders from any high-street coffee shop, he always asks for the same drink — one filter coffee, cold milk — and is always annoyed by the inevitable response:
"Regular?"
His reply never fails to perplex the sales assistant.
"No, thank you. Just the once."

**Andy Maby**
Reigate, Surrey

SIR — It seems I cannot go into a shop now without being:

(a) asked how I am today.

(b) instructed to have a great afternoon/evening.

I am often sorely tempted to recite my medical history in answer to (a) and to tell the inquirer I am on my way to a funeral in response to (b).

**June Green**
Bagshot, Surrey

# DAILY SPECIAL'S

SIR – I was in a pub recently while the Daily Specials board was being written.

When it declared "Cod, pea's and chips", I gently queried whether the apostrophe was correct. The scribe immediately apologised, rubbed it out – and added one to "chip's" instead.

**Bruce Denness**
Whitwell, Isle of Wight

SIR – Some years ago The Farmers Club actually held an Extraordinary General Meeting to ask members whether they wanted to be The Farmer's Club, The Farmers' Club or just The Farmers Club.

The last named was the outcome, but then I suppose farmers were too busy to read up on their punctuation.

**Warwick Banks**
Allington, Lincolnshire

SIR – For fear of being responsible for my dog's demise, I have yet to use the flea powder in my cupboard on which the label reads: "Kills fleas, lice, mites on cats, dogs and hairy pets".

**Janet Hanton**
Reading, Berkshire

SIR – In a recent article about the renaming of the Department for Culture, Media and Sport to the Department for Digital, Culture, Media and Sport, you suggest that grammarians might be exercised by a missing comma on the logo.

I think that most sensitive English speakers would be more concerned by the illiterate use of "Digital" as a noun.

**Andy Bowles**
London N19

# BRAND NEW ANNOYANCES

SIR — For some time now we've had no new television programmes to look out for: they're all announced as "brand new". Can somebody explain the difference?

**John Edmunds**
Rottingdean, East Sussex

SIR — Could someone please clarify the difference between "clear" and "absolutely clear"?

**Bob Best**
Weobley, Herefordshire

SIR — Why do the media now use "two times" rather than the far more elegant and familiar "twice"?

**Robert E. Lerwill**
Runwell, Essex

SIR — The battle against "I'm good" is irretrievably lost. Do we, however, have to adopt the latest horror from across the Atlantic: I'm done?

**Juliet May**
St Mary's, Isles of Scilly

# GOVERNING IN PROSE

SIR — Once, our statesmen soared with cadence, character and content. Now they are simply tense and turgid. Even Tony Blair was capable of a tricolon; the current Labour leader employs cumbersome prose as a mark of authenticity.

As Mrs May's government rushes to return to grammar schools, they should perhaps not neglect the other elements of the Trivium.

**John Oxley**
London E15

SIR — Can anyone explain where I might find the table everything seems to be put upon after the general election? It must be very large.

**Peter Alexander**
Fleet, Hampshire

SIR — What happens when a Parliamentary Whip defies the Whip? Self-flagellation, perhaps.

**Fiona Wild**
Cheltenham, Gloucestershire

# IDENTITY CRISIS

SIR — I don't think I'm of the "liberal elite", nor the "establishment", nor do I fit the profile of an "ordinary, decent working person".

Who am I?

**S.M.**
Teddington, Middlesex

SIR – Were I still an "ordinary working person" (I retired from teaching some years ago), I should find the title given by Jeremy Corbyn demeaning, patronising and insulting.

Why should a working person be "ordinary"?

**Shirley Page**
Caxton, Cambridgeshire

# THE JOY OF TEXT

SIR – I often think that if the voice telephone had been invented after text messaging, we would all have said, "What a great invention. We can actually talk to each other now instead of having to type out messages on this stupid small keyboard. Texting is dead."

If only.

**Bob Shacklock**
Onchan, Isle of Man

SIR – Experience has taught me this rule of thumb. Expect text replies from the young within two minutes, from the middle-aged within two hours and from the aged within two days.

**David Betts**
Reading, Berkshire

# HIGH OLD TIME

SIR – How does one qualify as a "high-class escort"? Does one just need to charge an exorbitant price?

This old lady from the sticks may need to know sometime.

**Christine Jones**
Corwen, Denbighshire

# INSULT TO INJURY

SIR – Can anyone explain why the words *pain* and *painful* have been replaced by *hurt* and *hurtful*?

**Tore Fauske**
Woodmancote, Gloucestershire

SIR – I shall be glad when *Febewary* is over. Many people don't seem to realise that there is a letter "r" after the "b".

**Dr Peter Law**
Cmwbran, Monmouthshire

SIR – "Migrants should learn English". So should the English.

**John Gibson**
Standlake, Oxfordshire

# ENGLISH AS SHE IS SPOKE

SIR – As a post-war immigrant, my late mother raised smiles with her quaint use of English. For example, asking bus conductors to tell her where she needed to "alight" for her destination, to which the answer was usually: "You mean tell you when to get off, love?"

I was reminded of that the other day when, in a slightly Nordic-sounding accent, the platform attendant at

Westminster Tube Station advised passengers to "Make haste! The train is now ready to depart."

**Andrew Kruszewski**
London SE12

SIR — I always thought the most frightening phrase in the English language is "replacement bus service".

**Ron Bryan**
Frizington, Cumbria

SIR — While waiting for a train, I heard an announcement on the tannoy: "For the convenience of passengers, no fighting will be allowed on the platform."

**Michael Joseph**
Lawford, Essex

SIR — Strange, the number of people who speak English across the world, yet suddenly forget it all when the aircraft boarding announcement is made.

**Mike West**
Eastleigh, Hampshire

# ALL-DAY BREXIT MENU

SIR — I understand that the hard Brexiteers aren't happy with the "hard" label. Perhaps consideration should be given to the names "Full English" or "Continental Brexit".

**Peter J. Jones**
Greenfield, Lancashire

SIR — Is there anything in between a hard Brexit and a soft Brexit, and if so what is it called?

**Peter Brown**
Stondon, Bedfordshire

SIR — Last week, in our Bed and Breakfast, a gentleman asked for a boiled egg.

My wife and I debated in the kitchen for a while whether he wanted it hard or soft boiled. We eventually decided and delivered soft. He actually wanted hard, but complained that we hadn't given him the option.

If only we had thought to ask in the first place.

**Richard Nash**
Conwy

SIR — I will crack open the Champagne when the BBC finally starts to talk of a "Brexit boost" rather than the "Brexit impact".

**Mike Truscott**
Falmouth, Cornwall

SIR — Our new aircraft carrier may be very modern and hi-tech — and no doubt its length is officially measured in metres — but it is very reassuring that the BBC newsreader described its length as "three football pitches".

This is what Brexit is all about.

**Philip Baker**
St Albans, Hertfordshire

# THE ANGLO-PHONE SONG
## CONTEST

SIR – If Jean-Claude Juncker is correct in believing
that English is losing its importance in the EU, why did
the majority of singers in the Eurovision Song contest,
including the German entry, prefer to sing in English?

**Tony Jackson**
Fulwood, Lancashire

SIR – The obvious language in which to negotiate Brexit is
German. Not only is that language widely understood in
Eastern Europe, it would also annoy the French.

**Michael Gorman**
Guildford, Surrey

SIR – If David Davis needs any help with his Brexit
negotiations, I have a dictionary of insults in four different
languages: German, French, Italian and Spanish.

The dictionary is 50 years old, so may not have fully
up-to-date colloquialisms, but it does contain such useful
French items as *balourd* (blundering idiot), *tête de mule*
(pig-headed), *foutaise* (nonsense) and *cretin bigleux* (cross-eyed
twit).

**Brian Powell**
Colchester, Essex

SIR – About 40 years ago, when living in France, I decided to go to the local evening class to learn Esperanto. I was welcomed in a very friendly fashion by the local French people, and at the halfway interval we all had a lively discussion about the possibilities of a worldwide language.

In English, of course.

**Liz Wheeldon**
Seaton, Devon

# HOME
# THOUGHTS ON
# ABROAD

# KOREAN BARBERISM

SIR — How can North Korea have the ability to produce an intercontinental nuclear ballistic missile, when there is no one in their country capable of giving Kim Jong-un a decent haircut?

**Brian Christley**
Abergele, Conwy

SIR — Japan has been holding exercises to prepare for possible conflict with North Korea.

One resident later said: "I was able to stay calm and evacuated in a few minutes."

That's understandable. I'd be fairly nervous too.

**Neil Russell**
Portsmouth

SIR — Apparently we're teetering on the edge of a new Cold War with Russia, potentially becoming a Hot War.

Still, look on the bright side. A Hot War would be over in a matter of minutes.

**Gabrielle de Pauw**
London N1

# BALANCE OF POWER

SIR — At least Donald Trump's presidency means that the world is a more balanced place — there are now nutcases in both the Kremlin and the White House.

**Andrew Callaway**
Northowram, West Yorkshire

SIR — Donald Trump: perhaps best described as "a bull in search of a china shop".

**John Stimpson**
Clanfield, Hampshire

SIR — It would seem that the Oval Office has gone pear-shaped.

**Rodney Chadburn**
Tattingstone, Suffolk

SIR — Apparently America will now end up with the "hump". Most teenagers do. Theirs is only a young country and I am sure they will get over this in the next four years or so.

**Judith A. Scott**
St Ives, Cambridgeshire

SIR — I'm 78 and have never been on a demonstration in my entire life, but were that dangerous idiot Trump to make a state visit to Britain, I'd be on the streets protesting — complete with walking stick.
Bad!

**Andrew Papworth**
Billericay, Essex

SIR — My mother, who, in her 93 years, has never shown the slightest interest in politics or current affairs, now awaits the evening news bulletin with bated breath, wondering what Mr Trump has done (or said) now. I can't decide if this is a good sign.

**Susan Bell**
Berwick-upon-Tweed, Northumberland

SIR – At least Donald Trump is doing something correctly – he always sports cufflinks.

**David Parry**
Farnham, Surrey

SIR – The reasonable man adapts himself to the world; the unreasonable one persists in trying to adapt the world to himself. Therefore all progress depends on the unreasonable man. Discuss.

**Simon Warde**
Bognor Regis, West Sussex

SIR – Relax. There is zero chance of Putin blackmailing Trump. Blackmail depends on the possibility of embarrassment.

**Allan Whittow**
Great Missenden, Buckinghamshire

SIR – You can tell what God thinks about money when you see the sort of people he gives it to.

**S. Lewin**
Northwood, Middlesex

SIR – As a matter of urgency, would you please commission Matt to explain, via a series of diagrams, the Trump hairdo.

**Lt Col I.R.M. Saker (retd)**
Shaftesbury, Dorset

SIR — Doesn't Donald Trump know it is extremely rude to point with a forefinger? He does it all the time — except when he is picking his nose.

> **Sue Pemberton**
> Bramham, West Yorkshire

SIR — It is a pity that Mr Trump won't immediately follow the example of that other germ-phobic tycoon, Howard Hughes, and become a recluse.

> **Ian McMullen**
> Doddington, Kent

SIR — It cannot be long before President Trump decides there should be a statue of himself at the White House, by popular demand.

> **Byron Matthews**
> Boston, Lincolnshire

SIR — Can anyone suggest the subject of conversation if Donald Trump, Jeremy Corbyn and Nicola Sturgeon were stuck in a faulty lift for an hour?

> **C.C.**
> Warnham, West Sussex

## THIRD AMONG EQUALS

SIR — Photographs of Mr Trump with his third wife remind me of an Army friend stationed in the US who attended a drinks party in Texas.

His host took him by the arm and led him across the

room to where a beautiful blonde young woman of about 19 was standing, saying: "Ah'd sure like you to meet mah sixth wife. Ah trades 'em in occasionally."

**Adrian Holloway**
Minchinhampton, Gloucestershire

SIR – Growing up, I was told my clothes should be tight enough to show I was a woman and loose enough to show I was a lady. Mrs Trump seems to have not heard the last bit.

**Hilary Jones**
St Mary Bourne, Hampshire

SIR – I will admit to thinking that Michelle Obama is possibly the most attractive First Lady ever, followed at a respectful distance by Gorbachev's wife.

I think I'm relatively safe revealing all as my wife tends not to read the Letters page.

**Fraser White**
Bunbury, Cheshire

SIR – I'm pretty certain there are a huge number of women who would agree with me that Barack Obama could wear a shell suit with socks and sandals and still look hot as hell.

**Angela Hanna**
North Aston, Oxfordshire

SIR – I recently asked my class of eight-year-olds: "Who is the First Lady?"

The answer came back: "Mary Berry".

**Piers Casimir-Mrowczynski**
Gustard Wood, Hertfordshire

# ASK NOT WHAT THE CIA CAN DO FOR YOU

SIR – President Trump is not the first American President to experience difficulties with his security services. In 1961, President Kennedy flew to Bermuda for a meeting at Government House with the Prime Minister, Harold Macmillan. On the first morning of his visit, the hot water in the President's room was cold.

It was discovered that, while checking the bedroom for listening devices, the American Secret Servicemen had turned off the immersion heater and forgotten to turn it on again.

When the President was told what had happened he replied, "The bloody Secret Service are always mucking up my life."

**Philip Wright**
London SW11

# IF YOU CAN MAKE IT HERE

SIR – A friend of my father's arrived as a young journalist in 1920s New York to find that he was able to afford only the most frugal accommodation.

There were just two rules: "No opium smoking on the stairs and carry out your own dead".

**Dominic Weston Smith**
Fernham, Oxfordshire

# THE GREAT WALL OF MEXICO

SIR – The estimated cost of building the wall on the Mexican border is 15 billion dollars. The President could consider a cheaper option: an army of unemployed, all-American artists could paint a Trump l'oeil of the Berlin Wall on a series of wooden-framed linen panels stretching from coast to coast.

**Dr Adrian Crisp**
Weston Colville, Cambridgeshire

SIR – Border controls are not new. It must be remembered that Heaven has a gate, a wall (or the gate is superfluous) and extreme vetting.

**Steve Cattell**
Hougham, Lincolnshire

SIR – Mexico may wish to pay for the wall after all – to curb migration in the other direction. Canada might want one too.

**Julian Pullan**
Bramley, Hampshire

SIR – The current Mexican pole vault record is held by Giovanni Lanaro at 5.82 metres – so 6 metres should do it.

**Keith Davies**
Telford, Shropshire

# TWIT-IN-CHIEF

SIR – The American President should be above any opinions expressed on social media. Had he learned anything other than acquiring property and money, he would have known what Abraham Lincoln said on the subject of attacks: "If I were to try to read, much less answer, all the attacks made on me, this shop might as well be closed for any other business."

> **Richard Seyd**
> Hawley, Hampshire

SIR – President Trump's latest tweet relating to "negative press covfefe" [sic] suggests he has moved on from fake news to fake words.

> **Kirsty Blunt**
> Sedgeford, Norfolk

SIR – I see Mr Trump's team have invented something called "alternative truths".
  George Orwell would have been so proud.

> **Bob Stebbings**
> Chorleywood, Hertfordshire

SIR – Are "alternative facts" the same as "unknown knowns"?

> **Mike Hart**
> Mannings Heath, West Sussex

SIR – How can I distinguish fake reports about fake news from real reports about fake news?

> **Allan Reese**
> Forston, Dorset

SIR — We learn that the Trump Administration has ordered that electronic devices may not be carried on flights from selected countries into the USA. Surely the most dangerous electronic devices on the globe, as demonstrated since the US presidential election, are those in the hands of Mr Trump himself?

**Philip Barry**
Lydden, Kent

# HANDS OFF THE SPECIAL RELATIONSHIP

SIR — I have often wondered what the term "Hands Across the Sea" meant. Now, having seen a picture of Donald Trump and Theresa May holding hands, I think I know.

**Anthony J. Cross**
Blackburn, Lancashire

SIR — Since the election of President Trump there have again been doubts raised about the "special relationship" between America and Britain. At a political level this may or may not be true, but at a more individual level may I offer this.

The night after the terrible fire at Grenfell Tower, we, as a 747 crew, were taxiing our aircraft to the runway for our return flight from Washington DC to London.

We were about to change controller frequencies when the ground controller transmitted:

"Just before you go, we know that London is going through a rough time at the moment. We want you to know that we are praying for you all. Godspeed for a safe flight home and God bless the Queen."

For such humanity to be displayed on a normally business-like air traffic frequency was very humbling and touching.

**Mark Arnold**
Frome, Somerset

SIR — Somehow I feel that President Trump would be seen as more respectful if he were to refer to Theresa May as "Mrs T" rather than "my Maggie".

**Andrew J. Smith**
Addington, Buckinghamshire

SIR — The 1944 pamphlet advising US troops on how to behave in wartime Britain, which is being re-published by the Imperial War Museum, was not the first of its kind.

I still have a copy of one given to my mother in 1943, which contains the following gem: "The British don't know how to make a good cup of coffee. You don't know how to make a good cup of tea. It's an even swap."

**Willie Montgomery**
Norwich

SIR — Recent news items have put me in mind of an apocryphal wartime Churchill story.

Before a meeting with de Gaulle, he was briefed about French greeting customs and warned that he might well be kissed on the cheek and expected to respond in kind.

His reply: "If it helps the war effort, I'll kiss him on all four cheeks."

**Nevill Swanson**
Worcester

SIR — I was disappointed to see Mrs May kissing the French Prime Minister. This is not a British custom, and it should not be encouraged. Nor did she manage to turn him into a handsome prince.

**Ged Martin**
Youghal, Co Cork, Ireland

SIR — Why do female politicians always have to be kissed? Did Margaret Thatcher have to endure this? I feel sorry for Mrs May and Mrs Merkel having to endure these embraces when a good handshake would be infinitely preferable.

Even in non-political circles, a man thinks he has to kiss a woman when first introduced. I wish he would not.

**Patricia Manning**
Epping, Essex

# END OF THE ENTENTE CORDIALE

SIR — When I first visited Paris a few years ago I was hoping to experience the rudeness for which Paris is so well known. I was disappointed to find that I had an enjoyable time without any such issues.

When I returned more recently, the hotel staff made absolutely certain that I would experience the worst customer service. Staff in well-known department stores were equally rude and unhelpful. When asking for directions I was given misleading information every time.

Having achieved my objective, I no longer feel that it is necessary to revisit this beautiful city.

**W.K. Wood**
Bolton, Lancashire

SIR – I have recently returned from my annual ski trip to France in desperate search of a vegetable. For yet another year I have attempted to teach our nearest neighbours that a lettuce leaf is not a salad.

I watched as victims of culinary ignorance consumed minced beef with no attempt to introduce it to the essence of cooking. Instead, the chefs rely upon a myriad of strange sauces to cover up their ineptitude and, I latterly realise, to disguise their real intent – of killing off the English.

Can anyone advise me as to how I can apply for a foreign aid grant to teach the French how to cook?

**Rory Holburn**
Bournemouth, Dorset

SIR – While sitting listening to a male blackbird in my daughter's garden in the Île-de-France, I realised that he was trilling a completely different set of notes from the English blackbirds in my garden.

Maybe he is trilling in French, à la Edith Piaf.

**Jane Wallen**
Tilston, Cheshire

# UPGRADING LE PEN

SIR — Four of the French President candidates, Fillon, Hamon, Macron and Mélenchon, have at least one thing in common: their names end in "on".

Might the other main candidate, Marine Le Pen, stand a better chance of winning if she changed her name to Le Crayon?

**Richard Symington**
London SW17

SIR — The forthcoming election in France pits polarised opponents against each other as the moderates shuffle lethargically away. One can only hope that the good folk of that beautiful country do not believe that Le Pen is mightier than the bored.

**Philip Merivale**
Keyhaven, Hampshire

SIR — Marine Le Pen is reported to have decided it was a mistake to canvass on the basis that France would leave the EU.

"Instead," said a spokesman, "we will renegotiate the EU treaties to give us more control over our budget and banking regulations."

That was David Cameron's idea, too.

**Brian Foster**
Shrivenham, Oxfordshire

SIR — One must congratulate Emmanuel Macron on being elected as the next President of France and for also being the youngest French leader since Napoleon I.

However, in progressing his desire for increased political union in Europe, Mr Macron would, perhaps, be wise to remember that the island of Saint Helena is still a British possession.

**Jonathan C. Simons**
Bishop's Stortford, Hertfordshire

# UNSINGED

SIR — I salute King Felipe. It is a brave King of Spain who visits England sporting a beard.

**Roger Pearce**
Corgnac sur l'Isle, Dordogne, France

# SYRIAN PEACE TALKS

SIR — The Syrian peace talks might be more speedily resolved if they were to take place in Aleppo, instead of Geneva. It would certainly concentrate the minds of the participants.

**Dr Paddy Fielder**
Brandeston, Suffolk

# LONG HAUL

SIR — I was surprised to read that Emily Thornberry, the shadow foreign secretary, thinks that food will go off if it is exported to Australia.

In November 1958 I sailed in the SS *Strathnaver* from the UK to Sydney. I was with a group of Royal Navy Petty

Officers going on loan to the Royal Australian Navy. There were a large number of "£10 Poms" on board, and in the hold was the first consignment of Birds Eye Fish Fingers bound for Australia.

While unloading in Sydney, a case of fish fingers accidently fell onto the quayside and burst open. I am pleased to say that they were not wasted, as the dockyard workers quickly picked them up and placed them in their pockets.

If that was able to happen in 1958, just think how much better moving food would be in the 21st century.

**Derrick G. Smith**
Bexhill-on-Sea, East Sussex

# GAUCHE DRIVING DECISIONS

SIR — The Mayor of Calais is proposing that, in order to welcome British drivers, they may be allowed to drive on the left. This reminds me of my time in Kenya in the late 1970s, when the country was considering switching from driving on the left to driving on the right.

There was much debate about the pros and cons and how the transition could be managed. The Members of Parliament considered, for some time, if it would be easier if lorries and buses switched to the other side of the road one week and cars the following week.

Finally, common sense won through, and nothing happened. Driving in East Africa was interesting enough at the time without the government introducing this initiative test.

**Paul Rutherford**
Bishops Sutton, Hampshire

SIR — I have often wondered how the left/right problem came about. Which bright spark decided to branch out first? And which side was first declared "the driver's side"?

**Jan Alcock**
Whalley, Lancashire

# THE ROADS
# MUCH
# TRAVELLED

# PASSING ON DRIVERLESS CARS

SIR — I live in an isolated hamlet with two miles of winding, single-lane road before the next village.

My question is this: when two driverless cars meet along this road, how do they know which should have to back to a passing place — if, indeed, they know where the passing places are?

**C.G.**
Kittisford, Somerset

SIR — I am yet to be convinced of the economic and social benefits of driverless cars. If, however, that is the way the world is going, I believe there is a compromise solution which does not put us all in thrall to the tech giants.

Why not design a vehicle which could hold 20 to 60 people, pre-programmed to carry out convenient journeys? The addition of a conductor to see people on and off, who could drive if necessary, would take care of safety. As the device would be universally available, we could call it an "omnibus".

**Phil Brennan**
Oxhill, Warwickshire

SIR — This absorption of the great planetary minds with driverless cars is all very well, but what I really need is a suitable vehicle to get me, my family and trappings to Mars.

**Mark Ellison**
Long Buckby, Northamptonshire

SIR – Having seen how vehicles are currently driven by people using hand-held devices, I believe that driverless cars are already on the roads.

**Claire McCombie**
Lower Ufford, Suffolk

SIR – I was recently overtaken on the M4 near Bristol at eight o'clock in the morning by a young lady eating a bowl of cereal at the wheel, spoon in hand.

**Rev Richard Fothergill**
South Stoke, Somerset

# ROAD RAGE

SIR – As I do not tweet, this is my wish for the person who put a dent in my car door at the supermarket this morning and left without leaving personal details. May the fleas of a thousand camels infest your armpits and your gearbox disintegrate on the motorway during rush hour.

**Brian Hart**
Appleton, Cheshire

SIR – Might I respectfully suggest to those who drive an oversized car, presumably to compensate for a lack of inner self-esteem, that by complaining about the size of parking spaces, they are in fact seeking an answer to the wrong problem.

**Rowland Aarons**
London N3

SIR – I often throw apple cores into country hedges from my car window.

Am I a bad person?

**David Watt**
Oakley, Buckinghamshire

# COMMUNITY SUPPORT

SIR – Many years ago I drove my bright red Mini to work along the same route every weekday. One morning the constable controlling a pedestrian crossing (those were the days) waved me down and asked to see my licence.

"I just wanted to find out your name," he said. "Will you come to a party tonight?"

**Anne Osborne**
Ringwood, Hampshire

SIR – I remember, as a trainee police constable at Hendon in 1960, instructors telling the cautionary tale of a street duty officer who stopped a car being driven by an oriental gentleman for passing a traffic light at red.

Officer: "When red showee, you no goee."

Driver, in perfect English: "Officer, I am the Chinese Ambassador to the Court of St James."

The outcome of this encounter is not known.

**George Holder**
London SW20

# MODERN JOUSTING

SIR – What is the umbrella etiquette when walking along crowded pavements? Does one lower, raise, tilt sideways or bash straight on?

**Veronica Timperley**
London W1

# BOULDER-DASH

SIR – When I was a schoolboy many years ago in rural Lancashire, I remember seeing a road sign warning drivers to beware of falling boulders. I have never managed to work out how to do it.

**Philip Goddard**
London SE19

SIR – I often see signs warning me of slow children but, though I always keep my eyes peeled, I have yet to find one advertising fast women.

**Owen Hay**
Stanway, Essex

SIR – I, for one, am very grateful for the helpful advice and encouragement that has started appearing on roadside signs in recent years.

Motorists, as they travel happily on their way, cannot fail to be inspired by messages such as, "Hey, let's all try to get home without crashing, shall we?" or, "Together we can beat congestion".

Further afield, such missives can open deeper philosophical issues. Having fed one's coins into the parking ticket machines at Shannon Airport, the weary traveller is offered a Delphic proposition: "Change is possible".

**Dr Tony Stroker**
Woodcote, Berkshire

# A NEW HUBBUB

SIR — The *Telegraph* included an artist's impression of what the proposed new third runway at Heathrow might look like with a ramp or platform crossing the M25 motorway.

Clearly the artist concerned has never been anywhere near this section of the motorway, otherwise they would have increased the number of motor vehicles shown by at least a factor of 20, with hundreds of traffic cones, hard hats and yellow hi-vis jackets thrown in for good measure,

**Ian Jenkins**
Hereford

# UNHENGED

SIR — Instead of an underpass or flyover to ease congestion, why not move Stonehenge? After all, it was stupid to build it so close to the A303 in the first place.

**Andrew Browne**
Chinnor, Oxfordshire

# CHERISHED PLATES

SIR — You report that the DVLA has withdrawn a number plate which seemed to spell "jihad".

The most intriguing plate I ever noticed was "HE5 GAY".

**Chris James**
Abergele, Conwy

# PARP, PARP, PARP!

SIR — Motor cars should be fitted with three different-toned horns. The first tone should be a danger warning: the original purpose of the horn. The second tone should have a friendly sound, which is used to wave at passing friends. The third selection would be a really harsh noise, which is used to show aggression when impatient.

**Bill McCreath**
Sheffield

SIR — In my youth, 45 years ago, I had a Klaxon horn fitted to my Triumph Spitfire car. It worked wonders travelling across Caldbeck Common, en route from Carlisle to Keswick, as it prevented the frolicking spring lambs becoming chops before their time.

**Patrick Tracey**
Carlisle

SIR — I have fond memories of the independence the "Noddy" car gave to my widowed and disabled mother. When we married in 1966 and she moved house, the little car went too — in the removal van. Even when she drove it through a neighbour's hedge and down a three-foot drop, they both came up smiling.

**Sue Suter**
Newton Blossomville, Buckinghamshire

## THOUGHT FOR TODAY

SIR — John Humphrys says that he does not need to wear a protective helmet when riding a bicycle as his white hair will cause people to avoid him. I trust that potholes will give him the same respect.

**Roger Hannaford**
Haddenham, Buckinghamshire

SIR — My wife and I, who both suffer from back pain, have a theory that road humps are sponsored by chiropractors.

**William Lawson Mills**
New Milton, Hampshire

## BOTTOM OF THE PILE

SIR — I remember reading a critic's report on the opening of a restaurant near Bromley in Kent a few years ago that commented: "Geographically it is halfway between Elmer's

End and Pratt's Bottom. Gastronomically it is about the same."

**David Shaw**
Codford St Mary, Wiltshire

SIR – The news that Hull is to become the latest European City of Culture (a contradiction in terms if ever there was one) reminds me of a comment made some years ago at a security conference I attended.

The chairman, head of security for the county of Cheshire, apologised to the delegates for the venue, which was situated in a very unattractive city overspill development.

He said: "How shall I put it . . .? If Cheshire was a human body, this is where it would get piles."

**Sid Davies**
Bramhall, Cheshire

# YOUR CARRIAGE AWAITS

SIR – For many of us senior citizens the realisation that we are entering the "third age" can be quite sudden. My own enlightenment came when an admiring glance at an attractive young lady on the London Underground did not produce the usual "get lost" look in response. Instead she got up and offered me her seat.

**Paul Corser**
Selborne, Hampshire

SIR – As I sit in the so-called "quiet carriage" from Cheltenham to Paddington, I simply cannot concentrate on my book for the quite deafening noise of people tapping on their laptop keyboards.

However, even more disconcerting is the realisation that my children are correct in that I have now officially joined the ranks of boring old farts.

**Ben Wright**
Kings Stanley, Gloucestershire

SIR – Are there more eccentrics on the London Underground than there used to be?

Yesterday I sat opposite a young woman who boarded the Bakerloo train at Oxford Circus and, with much joy, proceeded to strip naked from the waist up. Two American tourists looked uncomfortable but everyone else appeared not to have noticed.

**Margaret Roberts**
Rowledge, Surrey

SIR – Earlier this year, my friend and I were travelling around Ireland by train and we had reserved seats for all our main journeys.

It was St Patrick's Day and the train was packed with exuberant, excited and rather intoxicated young people. We found our seats and, not surprisingly, they were occupied by two young men.

Harry, my friend, said: "Excuse me, but these seats are reserved. We need to sit down; I am 87 and my friend is 84."

The reply was: "You've already lived too long – you should be dead."

**Dennis Gilbert**
Bradford on Avon, Wiltshire

SIR – I was on an utterly packed Tube train during the rush hour on a very hot summer's morning. We stopped outside Victoria and after a few moments the lights went out.

Resigned silence reigned, then a voice floated out of one end: "If everybody at the other end breathes in, we at this end can breathe out."

The ensuing laughter convulsed the entire carriage.

**Andrew Given**
Cranborne, Wiltshire

SIR – Outside church on Good Friday, I overheard one of our younger parishioners ask his parents if The Stations of The Cross had anything to do with trains.

I resisted the urge and temptation to suggest that, thank God, they were not, as had South West Trains or Southern Rail had a hand in the proceedings, we would all still be here next Wednesday.

**Nicky Samengo-Turner**
Newmarket, Suffolk

# NATIONALISING MR SOUTHERN

SIR — I was very alarmed to read on the front page of my *Telegraph* that I am about to be nationalised. I do not want to be in public ownership; I'm quite happy as I am.

> **Barry Southern**
> Sutterton, Lincolnshire

SIR — I now place train drivers in the same category as MPs.

> **Barrie Freeman**
> Yapton, West Sussex

SIR — In the days of slam-door coaching stock, we passengers were entrusted to open and close the doors ourselves.

Perhaps the problem of who operates the sliding doors on the Southern trains could be overcome by replacing the doors with passenger-operated curtains.

> **David Cable**
> Hartley Wintney, Hampshire

SIR — Thank goodness for the Internet, which still allows us to work and communicate, despite all this travel disruption. God help us if the artificial intelligence in all those data centres learns to unionise.

> **Iwan Price-Evans**
> London SW1

# THE 100-MINUTE MILE

SIR — Infrastructure projects like Crossrail and Hinkley Point are all very well and HS2 will reduce travel time from London to Birmingham to 49 minutes. This is quicker than the time it took me to travel half a mile on the Jamaica Road in Bermondsey the other evening. Have we got our priorities right?

**Tim Spurrier**
Brooke, Norfolk

SIR — If my home finances were in the same state as the nation's, I would not be considering buying a new train set just because it goes a bit faster than my current one.

**Tim Howard-Jones**
Salisbury

SIR — Cats as stationmasters are a good idea. They rarely miss any comings and goings. I have appointed my cat Fred as the stationmaster of our much-loved but unmanned station here in Bruton, Somerset. I hope there will be no objections.

**Mark Robbins**
Bruton, Somerset

# LEADING THE CHARGE

SIR — In the interests of saving both money and the planet, I have been considering the purchase of an electric car. However, until such time that recharging points are

installed in the car parks of gastropubs, I shall not be
changing for the time being.

**Philip Urlwin-Smith**
Chobham, Surrey

SIR – A welcome future development would be to electrify
all motorbikes. We would then be able to sit in our gardens
at weekends in relative peace, allowing the convoys of these
offending machines to continue to speed through our
village more silently.

**Dr Malcolm Clarke**
Meifod, Powys

# THE BATTLE OF HENLEY

SIR – When I lived near Henley-on-Thames, my otherwise
quiet weekends were often rudely interrupted by a pair
of aerobatistes from a local aerodrome practising their
dog-fighting skills in the clear blue skies above my secluded
riverside home.

When I eventually complained, for some strange reason
the Civil Aviation Authority thought it would be extremely
unsporting of me to add some realism to the aerial combat
by joining in with an Ack-Ack gun.

**Robert Warner**
Ramsbury, Wiltshire

# KEEP YOUR LEGS CROSSED FOR BA

SIR – Some years ago, when centralised computer systems were in their infancy, my wife was working for an American computer company. One day she was called out urgently to cover a problem at a computer centre for a large company. One operator on the main computer said that she had just crossed her legs and the computer system went blank.

On looking under the desk, my wife found the problem. The girl's high-heeled shoe had caught the power cable and pulled the plug out of its socket. Once the plug was back in, everything was well again.

Perhaps BA suffered a similar problem somewhere.

**T.E.L. Langford**
Milford on Sea, Hampshire

SIR – The way BA has been carrying on, blaming an apparently mythical power failure, with no back-up, anyone would think it was being run by the Labour Party.

**Richard Shaw**
Dunstable, Bedfordshire

# IN-FLIGHT ENTERTAINMENT

SIR – May I suggest some alternative ways of passing the hours on a flight now that laptops and iPads are banned? One chief executive I heard about used to while away the time and relax in First Class by working on his embroidery. Some may even consider reading a book.

**Bob Whittington**
Frant, East Sussex

# ANTI-SOCIAL
# MEDIA

# I'VE STARTED BUT I CAN'T FINISH

SIR — I have just watched *Celebrity Mastermind*. I have never heard of any of them. Am I leading a sheltered life, or am I qualified to become a High Court judge?

>   **G. Brown**
>   Stretford, Lancashire

SIR — After watching a number of special quizzes on television over the Christmas period I have concluded that my understanding of the term "celebrity" requires revision. I now believe that a celebrity is an unintelligent, strange-looking person you have never heard of.

>   **Dr A.D. Portno**
>   Quarndon, Derbyshire

SIR — If Lady Gaga is really serious about de-stigmatising the discussion of mental health issues, may I suggest that she chooses a less offensive *nom de guerre*.

>   **Rory Mulvihill**
>   Naburn, North Yorkshire

SIR — I have never watched *EastEnders*, listened to *The Archers* or eaten broccoli.

 I have no regrets.

>   **Peter Harrison**
>   Altrincham, Cheshire

## *ARCHERS* AT THE BAR

SIR – The judge whose lenient sentencing of the man found guilty of abusing his wife by making her drink bleach has created demands for better training of the judiciary in the area of domestic violence.

I suggest that a low-cost way to achieve this training would be to sentence the judge to listen to the Rob and Helen storyline in *The Archers*.

**Sarah Collins**
Guiting Power, Gloucestershire

## GOOD MORNING, PIERS

SIR – If Piers Morgan thinks getting up early to front *Good Morning Britain* is killing him, just think what it's doing to those who have to watch him.

**Leslie Watson**
Swansea

## PITTFALLS OF FAME

SIR – In the 1960s I was perpetually fascinated by the splits and reunions of Elizabeth Taylor and Richard Burton. I could never understand why my grandfather's generation was not gripped by the same absorption and found the whole business tiresome.

Half a century on, with the wall-to-wall coverage of Angelina Jolie and Brad Pitt, I now understand perfectly.

**Edward Thomas**
Eastbourne, East Sussex

SIR – If my husband were unfortunate enough to resemble the photograph of Brad Pitt in your newspaper, I would be inclined to divorce him on the grounds of looking like Herr Flick of the Gestapo.

**Sandra Hancock**
Dawlish, Devon

SIR – One delight the Clooney twins have to look forward to is being asked if they are identical. This often happens to me, and I usually reply that my twin sister's beard is a different colour.

**Richard Morris**
Harrogate, North Yorkshire

# DISC JOCKEYING

SIR – It is not only the BBC who have overpaid stars. I regularly listen to Classic FM, whose presenters feel it necessary to say, several times an hour, "This is Joe (or Joan) Bloggs".

Do they think we really care who is putting the CD on?

**John Jenkins**
Bath

SIR – I regularly listen to my local radio station and am very happy with it: after all, there can be few other places where one can hear adverts for "Cesspool Sid" and for mobile lavatories (tagline: "Your business is our business").

**Bill Davidson**
Balderton, Nottinghamshire

SIR – Should there ever be concern over the BBC's charter and what the BBC chooses to pay the artists who front its programmes, has any programme done more than *Strictly Come Dancing* to show the eternal, artistic relationship between a man and a woman, which is the wonderful constant on this planet?

Whoever generated this programme is a genius to whom humankind should be grateful. The programme is a beautiful reassurance of the essence and continuity of human life.

**Robin Colby**
Bickington, Devon

## FUNDING THE NHS

SIR – With the BBC spending so much time in our hospitals, whether reporting news or making programmes, might I suggest that 20 per cent of the TV licence fee is donated to the NHS.

**David Belcher**
Thatcham, Berkshire

## CLIPPING THE PIPS

SIR – I have invented a new game linked to the *Today* programme on Radio 4.

As we approach the pips on the hour, I find myself betting on whether or not the presenter will finish his or her announcement without clipping the pips.

This is a childish game, but it provides a little gentle relief from the continuing tedium of the general election, the never-ending speculation about Brexit and the latest drama involving President Trump.

**Colin Bower**
Sherwood, Nottinghamshire

## PANIC FATIGUE

SIR – I panicked about the referendum. I panicked about the Labour and Conservative leadership elections and the US presidential election. I panicked about the pound dropping, the FTSE 100 not dropping and the Russians sending an obsolete aircraft carrier down the Channel.

I blame 24-hour news. In the good old days they had to send a clipper from outer Mongolia, which took three months to get back to Blighty, so the intelligentsia could cough and splutter over their devilled kidneys long after it had all happened, and there was no need to speculate what might happen tomorrow, next week, next month or next year.

I am all panicked out.

**James Griffin**
Hayling Island, Hampshire

## FROM YOUR OWN CORRESPONDENT

SIR – I note we are hearing a lot from the "Diplomatic Correspondents" from news organisations. Could I suggest they also appoint "Undiplomatic Correspondents" to provide us with an unvarnished version of the story?

If he were to become available I think Boris Johnson would
be ideal.

**Ian Bell**
Chew Stoke, Somerset

# CAREERS FOR SNEAKS

SIR — Never a day goes by without some private report,
letter or memo being leaked to the press. Whistleblowers
abound, even when it seems hard to fathom why they have
felt the need to blow.

In these enlightened times, I wonder whether
whistleblowing is now covered by careers departments at
schools.

"Binns, you have always been a bit of a sneak. Have you
thought about a career in whistleblowing?"

"Just you wait, Sir, I'm going to tell my Mum what you
just said."

**Peter Thompson**
Leaked from address below
Sutton, Surrey

# G*** C*** H*** Q***

SIR — As a GCHQ radio officer, my daughter asked me
what I actually did.

I told her that when someone swore on television I was
the person who bleeped out the bad language so that people
would not be offended. This seemed to satisfy her curiosity.

**Ranald Omand**
Harrogate, North Yorkshire

# MAKE DO AND SPEAK ENGLISH

SIR – Why do I hear so many American voices whenever I turn on any channel on the television or on radio? What is wrong with good old English? Surely someone should introduce rationing.

**John Blatchford**
Midsomer Norton, Somerset

SIR – During the coverage of Trooping the Colour on the BBC I heard Huw Edwards refer to the ensign receiving the colour as a second lieutenant, pronouncing it *loo* rather than *left*.

Is this the End of Western Civilisation As We Know It?

**Kimball Bailey**
London SW15

SIR – I will happily donate £20 to a charity of their choice to the first interviewer to get Plaid Cymru leader Leanne Wood to say, on air, the word "bumblebee".

**Eddie Lodge**
Plymouth

SIR – I would like to recommend the newsreader Kathy Clugston for one of the highest possible positions in the BBC. She appears to be the only person who is able to pronounce the word *harassment* correctly.

**M.H.**
Stafford

SIR – Am I the only one who has a deep Orwellian feeling of unease whenever I hear a newsreader say "See you later"?

> **Dave Nash**
> Margate, Kent

SIR – Perhaps unbeknown to us, there is a covert BAFTA award for period dramas with poor lighting or mumbling dialogue that producers are striving to achieve?

> **James Thacker**
> Tanworth-in-Arden, Warwickshire

SIR – At last, a unified call for more clarity of diction from the BBC! Maybe now my wife will stop nagging me to wear my hearing aids.

> **Hugh Gill**
> St Lawrence, Jersey

SIR – Watching the BBC's tripe for old people this afternoon, I found a programme on rescuing elephants. I was delighted that, after years of struggling to cope with words of more than two syllables, these animals are now referred to as *eles*. No doubt they will be enrolling at *unis* very soon.

> **G. Brunt**
> Butleigh, Somerset

SIR – The title of the ITV drama *Harlots* brought to mind the fabled encounter between Margot Asquith, wife of the Prime Minister, and Hollywood star Jean Harlow.

Tired of the actress deliberately mispronouncing her name, the Prime Minister's wife reportedly replied: "No, dear, the T is silent, as in Harlow."

**Brian Orr**
Groomsport, Co Down

## DOCTOR WHO?

SIR – I nominate Jeremy Corbyn as the next Doctor Who. Whatever epoch he visits his ideas stay exactly the same, and the sonic screwdriver has a charmingly proletariat feel about it.

**Dr David Cottam**
Dormansland, Surrey

## BBC'S RIGHTS AND WRONGS

SIR – Concerns have been raised that the appointment of a former Labour minister may result in left-wing bias on BBC radio.

The words "stable door" and "bolted" spring to mind.

**Eugene Smith**
Harrow, Middlesex

SIR – In the lexicon of the news media the far right is anyone who didn't vote Labour.

**Robert Stevenson**
Cheltenham, Gloucestershire

SIR – "On the BBC [viewers] will often hear people they disagree with saying things they do not like," says Nick Robinson, quite reasonably.

However, if they support UKIP, Israel, Brexit, grammar schools etc. they will rarely, if ever, hear people they agree with saying things they like.

**G.P. Brown**
Norwich

# KNIGHTS OF THE ROUND TABLE

SIR – The current ethos of the presenters on the *Today* programme appears to be to ask guests a question, wait for a few seconds into the reply, then interrupt them with their interpretation.

The BBC could save so much time and money if they dispensed with guests altogether and just had a jolly round-table discussion propounding their own views.

**Veronica Copley**
London SE26

SIR – When watching the BBC news I am struck by the fact that, whenever the PM or a minister is shown leaving or arriving in Downing Street, there is a voice off-camera shouting out some inane question. This question is always (quite rightly) ignored.

Can anyone tell me who this voice belongs to? Does the BBC now have a Department of Stupid Questions, paid for from the licence fee?

**Peter J. Willis**
Coggeshall, Essex

SIR — Logistic considerations mean that we can't all rush to Westminster to shout juvenile inanities at politicians whenever something significant happens, even if we thought it a remotely sensible and productive approach.

How fortunate, then, that we can rely on the BBC's microphone-jabbing and jabberer-in-chief Laura Kuenssberg to embarrass everyone to great effect.

**Richard Weeks**
Felixstowe, Suffolk

SIR — The blame lies with the BBC for feeding Laura Kuenssberg on live wasps, the last of which she has not finished chewing as she goes on air. When she is to question anyone in Cabinet, they throw in a hornet.

**B.T. Wall**
Nottingham

SIR — As one of a batch of four geriatrics at present on a sailing holiday along the French coast, I write to inform you that we have decided that Ms Kuenssberg is to blame for everything that goes wrong on this trip, from gear failures to seasickness.

**Dick Holness**
Herne Bay, Kent

SIR – Say what you like, but I'd take Laura Kuenssberg's lovely Scottish lilt rather than Robert Peston's whining seesaw any time.

**Edward Thomas**
Eastbourne, East Sussex

SIR – Just when you think it cannot get any worse, Robert Peston grows a moustache.

**Leslie Watson**
Swansea

# A PLAGUE ON YOUR DRAMA DEPARTMENT

SIR – You ask: "Can *Poldark* ever recover from *that* controversial sex scene?"

I think we are correct to vilify the BBC Drama Department for portraying life as messy and confusing, characters as flawed, and, indeed, for presenting drama at all. They will soon be banned in every student common room in the land.

For example, in the next BBC production of *Romeo and Juliet*, Tybalt must be shown undergoing Anger Management Therapy, Mercutio must wear a hi-vis jacket, there must be no underage sex, and Romeo must resort only to medications properly prescribed by a registered practitioner.

**Michael Rolfe**
Cape Town, South Africa

# PRINCIPLED ROLES

SIR – The actress Emma Watson has refused to play
Cinderella because she only wants parts that portray suitably
empowered role models or people whose views "resonate
with her principles".

  She is fortunate to be in a position to be so choosy.
If other thespians adopt the same policy there may be a
marked decline in theatrical offerings. Lady Macbeth,
Queen Elizabeth I and many other major roles certainly
portray "empowered" women, but these women also had
a tendency to rid themselves of any opposition in a very
non-PC way.

**Sandra Jones**
Old Cleeve, Somerset

# THE BERMUDA FLOWER SHOW

SIR – I waited with eager anticipation for this year's Chelsea
Flower Show. After two days' coverage on the BBC I have
yet to see a rose, a delphinium or paeonia – or indeed any
other English garden flower.

  A Maltese quarry (which looks like an overgrown, weedy
cemetery), an interviewee who professes not to like flowers,
a look-alike climbing frame and a Bermuda Triangle – are
these the quintessentially English flower gardens I am trying
to achieve?

**Suzie Breakwell**
Sherrington, Wiltshire

SIR — I think there has been a mistake. Someone fly-tipped a load of old concrete blocks on a weed-infested wasteland in Chelsea and it won Best in Show.

**Barrie McKay**
South Cerney, Gloucestershire

SIR — Watching the Chelsea Flower Show on television is a bit like watching a porn movie. Everything on show is bigger and more impressive than mine, and leaves me feeling totally inadequate.

**Eric Wells**
Nottingham

# SOD OFF, SUE

SIR — Mary Berry and Sue Perkins, on leaving *The Great British Bake Off*, are considering a similar programme themed on gardening.

May one assume that it will be called *The Great British Sod Off*?

**Andrew Mortimer**
Watford

SIR — Are Mel and Sue the grammar school Ant and Dec?

**Michael Marks**
Glascwm, Powys

SIR – If Channel 4 are prepared to pay £75 million for a television programme, that works out at about £5 per viewer. I'd rather they just sent me a bag of doughnuts and a chocolate cake.

**Simon Shneerson**
Chorleywood, Hertfordshire

# THE ROUTE OF
# ALL HAPPINESS

SIR – In a recent BBC One documentary, the Metropolitan Police were shown using a "money dog" to locate cash hidden in a property. Where can I buy one of these dogs?

**Roy Hughes**
Marlbrook, Worcestershire

# MURDER THEY WROTE

SIR – Another series of *Midsomer Murders* comes to an end. Presumably they break to re-stock the village.

**Mark Rayner**
Eastbourne, East Sussex

# ALL OVER BY CHRISTMAS

SIR – The television schedules during the festive season listed, inter alia, the following:
   *Dunkirk* (twice)
   *Where Eagles Dare*
   *The Heroes of Telemark*

*Up Periscope*
*Kelly's Heroes*
*The Dam Busters*
*The Bridge at Remagen*.
What do Germans watch at this time of year?

> **John Layton**
> London SW13

# I'D LIKE TO THANK MY ACCOUNTANT

SIR – Congratulations to PwC – their little glitch at the Oscars ceremony ensured that the headlines weren't taken up with the stars' interminable thoughts on Donald Trump.

> **Judith Sutherland**
> Hale, Cheshire

SIR – As a Chartered Accountant, can I say how proud I feel that a member of our profession has done something interesting.

> **Keith Olding MBA FCA**
> Elstead, Surrey

SIR – Following *La La Land*'s success at the Oscars I look forward to its producers continuing with the Teletubbies theme, making the *Po Land* sequel.

Hopefully Tinky, Winky and Dipsy will not be presenting the awards next time.

> **Tim Fox**
> Beckenham, Kent

SIR – How appropriate that *La La Land* should fall victim to fake news.

**Mary Whitehead**
Hove, East Sussex

# THE FINAL COUNTDOWN

SIR – Television appears to be full of awards for "The Best of...". Following the passing of an increasing number of friends and relatives, I was struck by the efficiency and professionalism of the crematorium staff. Perhaps they too could have an award, possibly entitled *The Crem de la Crem*.

**Alan Cubbin**
Weasenham St Peter, Norfolk

# THAT'S NOT MY WEATHER

SIR – Weather forecasters on television and radio often finish with: "That's your weather."
Do they live in some Edenic world of their own?

**Timothy Sharp**
Wooler, Northumberland

SIR – Now that winter has arrived, could I please ask female weather presenters on television to refrain from wearing sundresses?

**Penelope Fairclough**
Handley, Cheshire

SIR – I do wish a warm, humid night was not described by weather forecasters as being "sticky". This is a revolting term. Do these weather people not have access to showers?

**Philip Cottier**
Dolphinton, Peebleshire

SIR – My mother described a certain kind of precipitation as "that wetting rain". We all knew what she meant.

**Jonathan Whittingham**
Bomere Heath, Shropshire

SIR – The first sign of high summer has arrived: a heatwave followed by a thunderstorm. I now await the final sign, which is always the French air traffic controllers' strike.

**Claire Mccombie**
Lower Ufford, Suffolk

SIR – As a pensioner, and by definition old and vulnerable, I feel sure my "cooling allowance" should have been triggered by now.

**Thomas W. Jefferson**
Howden, East Yorkshire

# ROYAL DISAPPROVAL

SIR – The Queen watches *Mrs Brown's Boys*? One is disgusted.

**Phillip Crossland**
Nafferton, East Yorkshire

SIR – Having watched all the instalments so far of *Victoria* on ITV, I can accept Jenna Coleman's picture-perfect prettiness – this is, after all, Sunday night television. However, I find it increasingly difficult to tolerate Tom Hughes's performance. Why the hang-dog expression, floppy hair and whispered delivery? How thoroughly un-Germanic.

**Jill Richardson**
Melton, Suffolk

# ROYAL BLUSHES

# IN THE CROSS HEIRS

SIR — The following scene is unlikely to appear in the Netflix drama *The Crown*.

In the late 1940s, my father, Gordon Hughes, did his National Service in the Fleet Air Arm. On guard duty in Portsmouth with his loaded rifle one snowy January night, he heard footsteps approaching. Pointing his rifle into the dark, he issued the usual challenge: "Halt, who goes there?"

Rather than the correct password, a commanding, imperious voice replied: "Out of my way, you bloody silly man" — and Lieutenant Philip Mountbatten strode into the weak light shining from the guardroom window.

My father thought he was probably the only person ever to have pointed a loaded rifle at Prince Philip. He always wondered, if he had been more zealous and diligent, how different the future of the Royal Family might have been.

**David Hughes**
Sevenoaks, Kent

SIR — I'm concerned: does the Duke stepping down at 95 mean that the government will now increase the retirement age for the rest of us?

**Rae Duffield**
Beddgelert, Gwynedd

SIR — May I take this opportunity to thank the Duke of Edinburgh for his service to the Queen and this country. Stupid old bugger.

**Gordon Everett**
Newbold on Stour, Warwickshire

SIR — Now that the Duke has time on his hands, perhaps he could accompany the Prime Minister on her Brexit negotiations.

**Les Hurst**
Dartmouth, Devon

# HAIRS AND GRACE

SIR — Prince Harry is a favourite of mine, and he was obviously a first-class soldier. However, he lets himself and his regiment down by wearing that growth on his chin. Hopefully his new girlfriend will tell him how scruffy it looks.

**Major Peter Horsfall (retd)**
London N14

SIR — It has become a tradition for gentlemen to participate in growing facial hair for Movember. Since so many, from cricketers to rugby players, television presenters to young royalty, have been sporting whiskers for most of this year, could I suggest that we might look forward to a new month, namely Re-movember.

**Judith Barnes**
St Ives, Cambridgeshire

SIR — With the beards and the very tight trousers, surely the next fashion statement by the chaps should be the codpiece?

**Mick Philp**
Lincoln

SIR — May I respectfully suggest that Prince Harry would enhance his smartness if he used a Windsor knot when tying his tie.

> **Carl Wimperis**
> Kenilworth, Warwickshire

SIR — Having had the young Royals featured on Radio 1, how long before they appear in *Coronation Street*?

> **David Wooding**
> Clapham, Bedfordshire

## ROYAL NAMESAKES

SIR — My father was called William. I was born in the early 1950s and, at the time, was the only Andrew in my village. One of my middle names is Harry. At the time, I lived not a world away from Windsor Castle.

Of my adult children, my son is called George and one of my daughters is called Katherine. Our house is only 15 minutes away from Holyrood Palace.

Is the Royal Family keeping an eye on us?

> **Andrew H.N. Gray**
> Edinburgh

## COURT CIRCULAR

SIR — In the 1970s, Prince Charles opened the Sports Centre at Stopsley, Luton.

One member of my tutor group took the day off to

attend. I put his reason for absence down in the register as "attendance at court".

**David Fleure**
Bromham, Bedfordshire

# PRETENDER TO THE THRONE

SIR — For my mother's 100th birthday we hired a Prince Charles lookalike. (We wanted the Queen, but she was extremely expensive.)

He duly arrived in a blue Jaguar, wearing an appropriate pin-striped suit, white shirt and military-looking tie. At the end of a family gathering in the garden, he appeared from behind some shrubbery and read a prepared speech, which included the card from his "mother", while fiddling occasionally with his shirt cuffs.

A most memorable day.

**William Fitzhugh**
Henley-on-Thames, Oxfordshire

# HM GOVERNMENT

SIR — I recently organised a greeting from the Queen for my parents' 60th wedding anniversary. The process was straightforward and communication from Buckingham Palace was courteous, swift and efficient.

Might we persuade Her Majesty to allow her Anniversaries Office to run the rest of the country?

**Deb Hancock**
Leatherhead, Surrey

# CRUISE MISSILES

SIR — While reading about our new aircraft carrier, I mentioned to my wife that HMS *Queen Elizabeth* had just been launched. She replied by enquiring if it was too late to book a cabin for the inaugural cruise.

I think a more belligerent sounding name would have been more appropriate for our biggest ever warship.

> **A.R. Belk**
> Leatherhead, Surrey

SIR — One hopes that if there is to be a new royal yacht, the powers-that-be will be able to deliver it more quickly than seems to be the case with railways, airports and power stations. Her Majesty is already over 90.

> **Derek Wellman**
> Lincoln

SIR — Following current trends in industry, surely the building of *Britannia II* will be undertaken by the Chinese, with British sources providing the propellers?

> **Adair Robson**
> Hawkhurst, Kent

# RE-FIT FOR A QUEEN

SIR — Her Majesty is to receive moneys towards urgent repairs at Buckingham Palace.

I understand the work will include plumbing.

Should Her Majesty be fortunate enough to find a

plumber who returns telephone calls, agrees to do the work and actually turns up to do the work, would she be kind enough to publish the contact number of said plumber in the Court Circular?

They have disappeared from this part of Norfolk.

> **Patricia Taylor**
> South Lopham, Norfolk

SIR – "Oh Mr Trump, we'd love to have you to stay, but I'm awfully sorry, we're having the builders in . . ."

> **Jennie Gibbs**
> Goring-by-Sea, West Sussex

SIR – As it is one of our country's most important buildings, it is right that public money should be spent on the upkeep and repair of Buckingham Palace.

Even so, however gracefully the occupants are ageing, it is time, surely, for them to consider downsizing.

> **Alan Thomas**
> Caerphilly, Glamorgan

SIR – If the Windsors do not wish to carry on, I am sure the Middleton family would be only too happy to take over.

> **John Wheeler**
> Gerrards Cross, Buckinghamshire

SIR – To help the Queen and Royal Family manage their increasing workload, my wife informs me she would be very happy to take on the Wimbledon patronage. To do my part, I'll offer to look after the England and Wales Cricket

Board, which leaves me the winter to help out with the Rugby Football Union.

**David Cartwright**
Woodborough, Nottinghamshire

# GOOD AND BAD
# SPORTS

# CHRIST AT THE COP

SIR – Your headline in the Sport pages, "Jesus fit again" reminds me of when, in the 1960s, Liverpool Football Club fielded a legendary forward line, including Arrowsmith, St John and Callaghan.

An evangelistic slogan had been painted in large white letters on a block of grim Liverpool Council flats: "What will ye do when Christ cometh to Liverpool?"

Below someone had added: "Move St John to midfield".

**Nick Marler**
Otley, West Yorkshire

# THE BEAUTIFUL GAME

SIR – On the train to Nelson I had the misfortune to be in the same carriage as away supporters travelling to the Accrington vs Portsmouth game. Why do we continue to tolerate drunk-before-lunch, loud-beer-can-chucking, foul-mouthed, knuckle-dragging Neanderthals grunting "Oo are we? Oo are we?"

Portsmouth supporters should note the previous paragraph for the answer to this philosophical question.

**Jeffrey Simon**
Lytham St Annes, Lancashire

SIR – As a former chairman of the Aspinall Foundation for 11 years, I had close contact with gorillas, both captive and wild.

I would far prefer to be compared to this wonderful beast than to any Premier League footballer.

**James Osborne**
Canterbury

SIR – A world without football is a secret fantasy of mine, not least because of the Botox and hairstyles.

**Catherine Lewis**
Ware, Hertfordshire

SIR – A member of my Fourth XI football team fell in the penalty area yesterday and the referee awarded a spot-kick to our team. The player involved told the referee that in fact there had been no foul and so the decision was changed.

We would welcome any visitors from professional football so that they can witness that the "beautiful game" is still alive and well in leafy Surrey.

**Mike Howard**
Cranleigh Prep School, Surrey

# ACT IT LIKE BECKHAM

SIR – It would seem that David "Brand" Beckham's debut on the silver screen has not been a raging success. I do find this surprising: modern footballers seem to spend so much of their time play-acting that I would have thought he'd have been an instant nominee for an Oscar.

**David Costigan**
Gosport, Hampshire

SIR — Why all this recent fuss and bother about David Beckham's unsatisfied desire to be knighted?

I have to say I thought he already had been — for services to Britain's tattooing industry.

**Simon Smedley**
Chilcompton, Somerset

## WAYNE STOPS PLAY

SIR — You've got to feel sorry for Wayne Rooney. Just when he's managed to learn the words of the National Anthem, he's dropped from the line-up.

**Roger Manning**
Taunton, Somerset

## HALF-TIME TALK

SIR — Can broadcasters please be a little bit more careful in choosing the adverts that they show at half-time in televised football matches? Watching in a crowded pub I, like many other customers, took advantage of the break to visit the men's room and found myself wedged between two complete strangers.

Our discomfort wasn't eased when the paper-thin walls failed to muffle a loud chorus of "Go Compare".

**Clive Pilley**
Westcliff-on-Sea, Esssex

# WALKER-PETERS TO MAITLAND-NILES TO CALVERT-LEWIN

SIR – While keen for the young stars of the Under-20 World Cup-winning football team to succeed, I do feel that, should the current trend in hyphenated surnames continue, many commentators will find themselves seriously challenged when describing a particularly fast phase of play.

**Keith Edwards**
Tattershall, Lincolnshire

# DANGERS OF SCHOOL SPORTS DAY

SIR – School sports days are dangerous. On one occasion at my son's prep school, the parental casualties included one rotator cuff tear, one torn Achilles tendon and one head injury. I suffered the last one, having bounced out of the sack.

**David Nunn**
West Malling, Kent

SIR – You report that the daredevil sport of parkour, in which participants leap between buildings, is set to become an official sport that could be taught in schools.

As long as they are not playing conkers while they jump, they should be safe.

**Janet Newis**
Sidcup, Kent

# GERIATRIC GAMES

SIR – As an octogenarian I should like to see the introduction of the Geriatric Games.

Events could include the 10-metre sprint, long-distance races of 50 and 100 metres, the low jump, the short jump, and so on.

There would be no drug testing as that would eliminate 90 per cent of the competitors. Sponsorship could be sought from companies such as Saga, Sanatogen and Horlicks. Admission would be free for all those too young to participate.

**Leonard Macauley**
Staining, Lancashire

# THE GODS OF CENTRE COURT

SIR – I learnt from the subtitles which accompany BBC television broadcasts from Wimbledon that the players are provided with "special souls".

Small wonder that some players become demi-gods.

**Robert Fromow**
London SW1

SIR – Overheard outside one of the gates onto Centre Court at Wimbledon: "Now, do you need the loo before we find our seats?"

"Mum, I'm 51."

**Jo Marchington**
Ashtead, Surrey

# BREAKING POINT

SIR — My wife has discovered that if she leaves the room, Andy Murray wins the point. For the sake of British tennis, should we go for separation?

**G.B.**
North Woodchester, Gloucestershire

SIR — Should the demand for the manufacture of gargoyles ever be resurrected, designers should look no further for their model than a profile of Andy Murray in triumph.

**Alan Anning**
Yateley, Hampshire

SIR — How long before Henman Hill is renamed the Konta Kop? Neither has quite climbed the mountain.

**Geoffrey Piper**
Parkgate, Cheshire

SIR — As we continue with our Brexit negotiations, I can't help noticing how sharp and well-disciplined our ball boys and girls are, compared to their French counterparts.

**Dr Peter Dallow**
Biddulph Park, Staffordshire

# ON THE HOOF

SIR — There is a problem with horse racing on the flat: invariably the fastest horse wins. This problem could be cured if in the middle of each race, the stable hands had to change the horse's saddle. That would add the necessary uncertainty and make the efficiency of the non-riders an important element in the outcome of any race.

I should sound a caution. The intellectual property in this brilliant idea may belong to Formula I.

**Geoffrey Woolhouse**
Griston, Norfolk

# GET YOUR COAT, YOU'VE SCORED

SIR — Proper score books have played an important part in my life.

I met my husband while scoring at a cricket match. The man who introduced us said: "You'd better watch him, he's an accountant."

**Shirley Fitton**
Morpeth, Northumberland

# GENTLEMAN'S GAME

SIR — How much better the world would be if the Germans had learnt to play cricket. A few important Test Matches would have distracted them from the rather disagreeable habit of duffing up their neighbours from time to time.

**Liz Saunders**
Eastbourne, East Sussex

SIR — How can Henry Blofeld possibly want to be hit on the head with a baseball bat if he becomes a burden to others?

It must be obvious that, if such a thing has to be done, then nothing other than a cricket bat should be used.

**Su Sainsbury**
Sunbury-on-Thames, Middlesex

# BOLT FROM THE BLUE

SIR — It is rumoured that the sprinter Usain Bolt is seeking a secondary sport. May I humbly suggest that he tries his hand at playing the game of croquet to enable him to wind down gently?

Croquet is a combination of skill, tactics and a slice of cunning, played by a wide number of people of most ages.

I can just visualise Bolt in his signature pose, crouching with one arm pointing skyward, the other clutching two large croquet balls, having knocked champion players such as Reg Bamford, Robert Fulford and Stephen Mulliner off the national and world rankings.

Surely a front-page picture scoop?

**Stephen Scrase**
Wakes Colne, Essex

# A BRIDGE TOO FAR

SIR — Now that those in authority have deemed that the card game bridge is a sport, will the bridge column be appearing in the Sport section of your newspaper?

**Robert Ward**
Loughborough, Leicestershire

# DEAR
## *DAILY TELEGRAPH*

# DEAD LINES

SIR – I find reading the newspaper so depressing these days. It is only when I turn to the obituaries that I start to cheer up.

**Victor J. Llewellyn**
Hingham, Norfolk

SIR – The songs of Leonard Cohen are intense, bitter-sweet and uplifting. He was the sinking man's Bob Dylan.

**John Riseley**
Harrogate, North Yorkshire

SIR – Back in the 1990s, my local pub ran a sweepstake for celebrities reaching the pearly gates, which was known as the stiffstakes.

After selecting a celebrity at random, payment was 50p per week until payout. The only rules were that there had to be an obituary in *The Daily Telegraph* and if there were more than one death on the same day it would be a Dead Heat and the pot shared.

It was 18 months until the first (and only) substantial payout.

**David Bedford**
Guildford, Surrey

SIR – I cannot stop myself checking the Ws in the Deaths. I seem to need reassurance that I am still present.

**Diana Whiteside**
Berkhamsted, Hertfordshire

SIR – Apologies to everyone who put out their flags, bunting and booked a marching band; I am still alive and as facetious as ever.

**Roger Moor**
Rustington, West Sussex

SIR – The three main subjects on your Obituaries page today were younger than me. Ah well.

**John Adam**
Blackpool

SIR – A nice bunch of obituaries today. Age range: 96–104.

**John Glasson (age 80)**
Stanton Lacy, Shropshire

SIR – It is very satisfying to read in the Deaths column that virtually all those named passed away "peacefully".

How does one pass away "noisily"?

**D.P.**
Hemingford Abbots, Cambridgeshire

# SILENCE IN HEAVEN

SIR – If the late Howard Hodgkin, whose infantile daubs you so reverentially reviewed, happens to bump into, let us say, Rembrandt, Canaletto or Vermeer on his arrival on the other side, will they have anything to talk about? I think not.

**Maurice Tripp**
Horton Kirby, Kent

## SYLVESTRE'S ONE LIFE

SIR — I understand that it is a journalistic foible to print someone's age after their name for no apparent reason, but surely your report about the cat poisoner in south-west France went a bit far in describing the sad demise of "Sylvestre, 10"?

**Richard Light**
Hitchin, Hertfordshire

## NO SYMPATHY FOR
## THE OLD DEVIL

SIR — In the light of your recent reports about Mick Jagger's activities, next time he tells you he "can't get no satisfaction", don't believe him.

**Richard Walker**
West Malvern, Worcestershire

## HAPPY SOLUTIONS

SIR — Many years of fostering small children have taught me an infallible way of dealing with a childish tantrum: pick up *The Daily Telegraph* and start filling in the crossword.

**Hazel Wyld**
Freshwater Bay, Isle of Wight

SIR – I have recently been on a prolonged course of steroids, the dose being increased significantly for three days every three weeks to cover a chemotherapy infusion. During those three days, I found that my ability to solve clues in *The Times*' cryptic crossword was significantly improved. I put it down to chance.

However, at lunch with my good friend Michael Garvin, sadly recently deceased, he proffered the quite spontaneous and unsolicited information that he had been suddenly and unusually able to complete the *Telegraph* crossword during the days that he was on high doses of steroids as part of the treatment of his cancer.

I promised to write to you, presuming that this is a well-known phenomenon, to enquire as to whether the competitors in your crossword competitions are subjected to routine testing for performance-enhancing drugs. Are they?

**Ian Fergusson**
Tillington, West Sussex

SIR – As a Sudoku addict, I will grab any discarded paper if it offers a quick fix.

What puzzles me is the disparity in the levels of difficulty posed in various papers. The one that gives me most pleasure is a certain feeling of superiority over our *Times* friends. When faced with a Super Fiendish in that rag, I almost always complete it – whereas in the *Telegraph* I am frequently challenged by the merely Tough, and always by the Diabolical.

**Sue Cooper**
Upper Hartfield, East Sussex

## STEERAGE CLASS

SIR – In the Merchant Navy it was common practice
for seafarers joining their ship overseas to bring a few
newspapers for their shipmates with them when flying out
from the UK. However, many seafarers, particularly the
younger ones, were skint by the end of their leaves and,
rather than buy newspapers, would linger before departing
their aircraft in order to hoover up those left on passenger
seats. Normally this meant *The Daily Telegraph* for the captain,
the *Daily Mail* for the chief engineer, the *Daily Mirror* for the
purser and the *Sun* for the bosun.

With the greatest respect to those other august
publications, the *Guardian* and the *Observer* were left lying
where they lay. Junior seafarers hoping for a pleasant voyage
know the difference between a bowline and a noose.

**Peter J. Newton**
Chellaston, Derbyshire

## FAMILY PAPER

SIR – My late father, a 1914–1918 war veteran and a British
Lions rugby player in the 1920s, always called his *Daily
Telegraph*, "The Telewag".

Please don't ask me why, but to this day all members of
my extended family still buy their *Telewag*s.

When abroad in my favourite bar in the Vendée, France,
I download my *Telewag* on free Wi-Fi. Got to keep in touch.

**Richard Davies**
Monmouth

# KEEPING UP APPEARANCES

SIR — Would it be possible to update the photos of article writers?

Some seem to enjoy the blessing of eternal youth, but when one sees them in another setting they look like their fathers or mothers. Quite a shock at the breakfast table!

**Adrian Markley**
Salisbury

SIR — How is it that Fraser Nelson has not aged at all in the last 20 years? Does he have a painting in the attic?

**Don Edwards**
Manningtree, Essex

SIR — I certainly enjoy reading Michael Deacon's sketches and his "On Saturday" column but am becoming increasingly puzzled.

Does he shave his beard off on Friday night, ready for his Saturday column, only to grow it again on Sunday, ready for his Monday morning sketch?

**Geoffrey White**
Wellow, Somerset

# SALES PATTER

SIR — While I do not admire full-page advertisements in your newspaper I do appreciate that without them I would pay more — or indeed not have a *Telegraph* to read at all.

So, if I must be faced by a young lady apparently dressed

only in perfume and lipstick, could you at least persuade her to smile and be cheerful?

**Bob Broughton**
Laleston, South Wales

SIR — How many more times do you propose to displace your popular Weather and Crosswords page with an advertisement featuring a young lady with a somewhat disagreeable expression, and advertising a perfume by Louis Vuitton?

If this letter does not appear on your correspondence page I shall assume that the young lady in question is related to the editor.

**S.D. Harris**
Puddletown, Dorset

SIR — You are advertising leather shoes in a deal of buy one, get one free. What has happened to the old-fashioned way of selling them in pairs?

**Kit Carson**
Budleigh Salterton, Devon

SIR — I see that an advertisement in the *Telegraph* is offering 25 per cent off women's clothing. I know which 25 per cent I would like removed.

**Max Bowker**
Swallowfield, Berkshire

SIR — The *Telegraph* today carries an advert for a leaf blower. Please, do not buy one.

**Alan Sabatini**
Bournemouth, Dorset

# THE LETTERS EDITOR WILL SEE YOU NOW

SIR – It appears the crisis in NHS waiting times can be laid squarely at the door of *The Daily Telegraph*'s Letters page. On Friday alone three letters from doctors were published. Banning letters from GPs would clearly free up more time to see patients.

**R.B.**
Bishop's Stortford, Hertfordshire

# BRAGGING WRITES

SIR – For some years now I have been corresponding with Robert Whittle on the subject of family history.

We have had many convivial telephone conversations, but have never met until today when we were brought right next to each other on your Letters page. The coincidence sparked another delightful telephone chat.

Another coincidence is that one of your regular contributors, Lesley Thompson, lives several doors down from me. With gritted teeth, she has just presented me with a copy of your latest Letters book, *Stop the World I Want to Get Off*.... She has two letters in the book and I have three. She is still talking to me, but only just.

**David Brown**
Lavenham, Suffolk

SIR – Last autumn I received a letter from Mr Hollingshead to say that one of my unprinted letters would be published in his latest book. Having purchased his book this week and read it from cover to cover, hoping to find my name in print at last, I find that I have been rejected again. Is this the end of life for me?

**Sally Dubuis**
Wareham, Dorset

SIR — Never let it be said that the fair sex do not have opinions to give to *The Daily Telegraph*.

I fire off a letter almost every week when something stirs me up and over some 50 years I have had three letters published.

My husband reckons the editor says, "Oh, it's that batty woman from Melbourn again", but I think my letters are just too pertinent to be used.

**Mavis Howard**
Melbourn, Cambridgeshire

SIR — Apart from a boyish desire to show off, men write to newspapers to make up for their inability to communicate normally.

**David Miller**
Tunbridge Wells, Kent

SIR — After sending in literally hundreds of letters to *The Daily Telegraph* over the decades, I have never had the honour of having a single one accepted. My wife sent her first one in yesterday and there it is in today's paper. My credibility within the family now lies in tatters. That's it; I give up.

**Jon Swainson**
Cambridge

SIR — I have had one long and serious letter published in 2004 but in the last few years have had more success with five short and mildly humorous letters.

Most of these have been sent late in the day but before succumbing to the lure of the corkscrew.

**Hilary Jarrett**
Norwich

SIR — Given the kudos that attends the publishing of one's letter, could not the occasion be marked by the issue of a lapel badge, along the lines of the much-coveted *Blue Peter* badge?

These awards could be colour coded to indicate the extent of the wearer's success rate.

If you are receptive to this idea I don't mind being the first recipient.

**Ray Cattle**
Wateringbury, Kent

SIR — Relieved to see Jane O'Nions back on your Letters page — I thought perhaps she had defected to *The Grauniad*.

**Steve Thomas**
Brackley, Northamptonshire

SIR — Please publish this letter. My friends John Stephen and Tony Parrack regularly have their correspondence in print and I feel somewhat excluded.

**Peter D. Webster**
Thornham Magna, Suffolk

SIR – The first letter I ever had published in *The Daily Telegraph* several decades ago described how I regarded my voting at elections as being secret, even to the extent of studiously ignoring requests for my polling card number or name from tellers posted outside the polling station.

The following day I received a furious letter from my *Telegraph*-reading spinster aunt describing the lengths she went to, as an ardent Conservative and active teller for a permanently Tory seat, to ensure that known party supporters turned out to vote. She finished her missive by stating that, as her only nephew and sole beneficiary, she had now cut me out of her will.

On her demise many years later it transpired that she had kept her word.

**Robert Warner**
Ramsbury, Wiltshire

# FILL IN THE BLANKS

SIR – Although I am a regular reader of *The Daily Telegraph* I am having increasing difficulty understanding words which are frequently transliterated with dashes or asterisks.

I think I know what f\*\*\* means but what is f---? Is it an alternative spelling of the same word, or some new vulgarity? I have no way of knowing what p\*\*\* means. Is it as bad as f\*\*\* or f--- or, worse, t---?

Could we perhaps have a short dictionary sent in a plain brown wrapper to those over 18 years of age?

**J.D. Morgan**
Beaconsfield, Buckinghamshire

SIR — I am having increasing trouble decoding your deleted expletives. Should I congratulate myself on the purity of my mind, or should I worry that I am out of the loop?

**Janet Kay**
Acomb, North Yorkshire

## PRICE WORTH PAYING

SIR — If I subscribe to Telegraph Premium, will the advertisements for Nigel Farage go away?

**George Land**
Sandiway, Cheshire

## YESTERDAY'S NEWS

SIR — I always read the newspapers the day after they are published. That way, with a considerable degree of smugness, I can say to myself: "I'm so glad this sort of thing is not going on today."

**Mike Spragg**
Great Yarmouth, Norfolk

## TOMORROW'S FIRE PAPER

SIR — Although my interest in sport is rather less than zero, the *Telegraph* Sports section is always the first part of the paper that I open on these cold winter mornings.

Its compact format and weight are perfectly designed for kindling the drawing room fire. Please don't change it.

**Charles Jackson**
Hyssington, Montgomeryshire

SIR – I find a single edition of *The Daily Telegraph* to be the perfect size and thickness to line the bottom of my chicken coop. Whether the three birds also enjoy the content is a matter of speculation.

**Andrew Griffee**
Stanford Bridge, Worcestershire

SIR – A nearby oak tree has produced the largest amount of acorns in the 15 years I've lived here – to the point they were bouncing off my head on my way to collect my *Daily Telegraph*. Some are at least 5cm long and as my thatch is rather thin these days, the paper proved a very useful shield on my way back home.

**Patrick Tracey**
Carlisle

# THE MATT DISCOUNT

SIR – As Matt is away at present, please advise how I apply for a partial refund of the cover price?

**Keith Young**
Woking, Surrey

# P.S.

Dear Iain,
Vanity impels me to be chuffed yet again to receive letters
from you seeking permission to include contributions in
your next book. Thank you once more for the compliment.
Any objections? Are you kidding?

Are you running out of titles yet? If so, how about: *Say
What You Like, But...* or *I'm Not Trying to Be Funny, But...*

Good wishes and good luck.

**Edward Thomas**
Eastbourne, East Sussex


Dear Iain
I'm sure I'm delighted that one of my missives should be
rowing for Goldie. Of course, I'm intrigued to know which
one (sigh, there are so many).

Nihil obstat.

**Ged Martin**
Youghal, County Cork, Ireland


Dear Iain,
Thank you for your letter.

I cannot think of any of my unpublished letters (an
uncomfortably large number) that should not be published
in your forthcoming book.

Your letter was not wasted; I shall of course buy the book.

I am long retired but very busy. I have read the *Telegraph*
since 1957 when I served in the RAF in West Germany.

It concerns me not that 95 per cent of my letters are
unpublished; once written, my mind is cleared.

Best wishes,

**Barry Bond**
Leigh on Sea, Essex